Jain Way of Life

A Guide to Compassionate, Healthy, and Happy Living

Editor: Yogendra Jain
Art Director/Designer: Preeti Jain, Boston, MA
Published by: JAINA (Federation of Jain Associations of North America)

Editor and Writer: Yogendra Jain, Boston, MA
Art Director/Designer: Preeti Jain, Boston, MA

Content contributors and reviewers:
Preeti Jain, Asmi Sanghvi, Megha Doshi, Elaine Kordis, Pravin Shah, Dr. Shantilal Mohnot, Dr. Vinay Jain, Anita Jain, Shilpa Shah, Priyanka Jain, Umang Jain, Rakesh Soni, Metri Jain, Chintan Shah, Sapna Jain, Sonia Shah, Ashini Shah, Tarla Dalal, Laxmi Jain, Dr. Manoj Jain, Yogesh Kamdar, Dr. Jina Shah, Dr. Vastupal Parikh, Sudhir M. Shah, Anita Shah, Paras Doshi, Finale Doshi, Nirav Shah, Prakash Teli, Apurva Patel, Kirit Daftary, Anop Vora, Archit Shah, Tarang Gosalia, Soha Shah, Dhara Shah, Pankaj Shah, Shardule Shah, Shrenik Shah, Neel Vora, Sunit Jain, Prem Jain, Dr. Sushil Jain, Pradip Shah, Darshana Shah, Tarachand Jain, Gunmala Jain, Shitul Shah, Dr. Sulekh Jain, Parimal Pandya, Dharmaraj Khot, Mayur Shah, Rasik Vagadia, and many reviewers and contributors.

In addition to the above contributors' original writings and analysis, some of the content was from Jain teaching material and online content. Best efforts have been made to acknowledge the authors, content, and source of information.

Printed in China.
Distributed by: JAINA (Federation of Jain Associations of North America) in coordination with JAINA Long Range Planning/ Leadership Commitee. July 2007.

Library of Congress Cataloging-In-Publication Data
Jain, Yogendra
Jain Way of Life, *A Guide to Compassionate, Healthy, and Happy Living*
Jain Way of Life by / Yogendra Jain - 1st ed.

ISBN 978-0-9773178-5-1
1. Jain. 2. Jainism. 3. Non-Violence. 4. Ahimsa 5. Compassion. 6. Interfaith. 7. Way of Life.
I. Title

Please send your comments and suggestions to: Yogendra Jain, yokjain@yahoo.com, www.jwol.org
To order this book and related materials, visit www.jwol.org

Essence of Jain Way of Life

Jainism is a religion and a way of life. For thousands of years, Jains have been practicing vegetarianism, yoga, meditation, and environmentalism. Jains have three core practices: Non-Violence, Non-Absolutism, and Non-Possessiveness (Ahimsa, Anekantvad, and Aparigraha – AAA).

Non-Violence is compassion and forgiveness in thoughts, words, and deeds toward all living beings. For this reason, Jains are vegetarians.

Non-Absolutism is respecting views of others. Jains encourage dialog and harmony with other faiths.

Non-Possessiveness is the balancing of needs and desires, while staying detached from our possessions.

Jains believe in the existence of a Soul – in each living being – which is eternal and divine. JAIN WAY OF LIFE (JWOL) respects and honors all living beings through the practice of Non-Violence, Non-Absolutism, and Non-Possessiveness. We are all interdependent and, by living a JAIN WAY OF LIFE (JWOL), we can bring peace and spirituality to our lives and to those around us.

Table of Contents

Table of Contents

Preface

Babies are not born with a user's manual, though sometimes we wish they were. Marriage does not come with a conflict resolution kit, though we wish it did. Dealing with life's problems is not easy, though thousands of generations have gone through trial and error—learning from previous generations.

Scriptures, may they be the Bible, Koran, Gita—or for Jains, hundreds of scriptures—have guided billions of people in achieving spiritually fulfilling lives. But these texts date back more than 2,000 years, and though the core principles still hold true, much has changed in the world.

For Jains the core principles are as simple as the triple A's: Non-Violence (Ahimsa), Non-Absolutism (Anekantvad) and Non-Possessiveness (Aparigrah). The challenge is applying these principles in an age of the Internet, cell phones, animal testing, global warming, and cultural and religious openness. In ancient times the choices were minimal; faith was strong. The choices in foods, travel, friends, places of worship, books, teachers, and professions were extremely limited. By contrast, the present day world is diverse, complex, ever-changing, and vibrant. Indeed, at every juncture one faces hundreds of choices. The very faith and actions that remain instinctive and unquestioned in India face intense scrutiny by teenagers and young adults in North America.

I know these difficulties first hand; I grew up in America, studied in grade school and college, and am now married with teenage children. Undeniably, the responsibility of parents to raise children in North America—the melting pot of the world—can be daunting. In order to help them and future generations embrace and adopt the Jain philosophy in their daily lives, I have written and compiled this book, *Jain Way of Life*. This book is an instruction manual, providing guidance on compassionate, happy and healthy living.

Jain Way of Life includes more than 50 chapters on such topics as "24 Reasons to Believe in and Live a Jain Way of Life," "Treasures in Jainism," "How to Raise a Jain Child," "Excelling in the Workplace," "Guidelines for High School Students," "The Art of Dying," as well as simple introductions into Jain Philosophy, Celebrations, Pujäs, Symbols, and History. This book makes the connection between us, our world, our faith, and the universal core values of the triple A's. Many of my students at the Jain Center of Greater Boston Pathshala and others throughout North America have contributed to this book.

This *Jain Way of Life* aspires to be the handbook for people from all walks of life, diverse backgrounds, and differing faiths. Please share your comments, experiences, and feedback. Many of us have made this book our personal user's manual. Our wish is that you will consider doing the same.

All proceeds from this book are donated.

Yogendra Jain
Boston, MA - August 2007

LIVE AND LET LIVE

Jainism Simplified

What is Jainism?

Jainism is a religion of Non-Violence (Ahimsa) propounded by a "Jin" i.e., the spiritual victor. The principles enunciated by a "Jin" constitute Jainism and the followers are known as "Jains." Jainism represents a symbiosis of the religious and scientific approaches, for better living based on the foundations of non-violence, peace, compassion, and humility toward all living beings. Jainism is the union of personal independence with social and ecological interdependence, and believes in harmony and love toward all living beings. For millions of Jains who have been practicing Jainism all over the world, it is a way of life! The central themes of the Jain Way of Life (JWOL) are:

• **Non-Violence (NV/Ahimsa)** promotes the autonomy of life of every living being. If you understand and believe that every Soul is autonomous, you will never trample on its right to live.

• **Non-Absolutism (NA/Anekantvad)** strengthens the autonomy of thought of every individual. If you perceive every being as a thinking individual, you will not trample on his or her thoughts and emotions.

• **Non-Possessiveness (NP/Aparigrah)** supports the autonomy of self-control, of striving to balance our personal consumption of things by rationalizing between our needs and desires. If you ultimately feel that you own nothing and no one, you will not trample the ecology on which our survival depends.

The most fundamental principle of Jainism is the concept of Non-Violence (Ahimsa). Therefore, Jainism has based its ethical code entirely on the observance of the tenet of non-violence, and hence it is said – "Ahimsa Paramo Dharmah" meaning "Non-violence is the supreme religion." The Jain dictum, "Parasparopagraho Jivanam" means "Souls render service to one another." It emphasizes the balance and harmony both among human beings, and between humanity and all other forms of life. Jains actively reflect on these values and incorporate them in daily practice. Specifically, they are strict vegetarians, minimize the use of leather, silk, and animal products, and manage their households so as to minimize harm to even insects and other small living beings. In addition, Jains engage in business practices which involve fair treatment of employees, buyers, suppliers, and they practice philanthropy.

Jain values of non-violence, compassion, tolerance, and humility are extremely relevant in the world today.

History of Jainism

Jainism is one of the oldest living religions, predating recorded history. It is an original system, quite distinct and independent from other systems of Indian philosophy. The term Jain means followers of the "Jinas" (Spiritual Victors), human teachers who attained omniscience through their own personal efforts. There have been 24 such Spiritual Victors (also known as "Tirthankars") and Mahāvir was the last of these.

Mahāvir (The Great Hero) was born 2,600 years ago in 599 BCE. At the age of 30, he left home on a spiritual quest. After 12 years of austerities and meditations, he attained omniscience. At age 72, Mahāvir left this mortal world and attained Nirvana, that blissful state beyond life and death. Mahāvir was not the founder of Jainism. He consolidated the faith by drawing together the teachings of the previous Tirthankars and by emphasizing the principles that are important for our time.

Jain Practices

Jains believe that to attain enlightenment and ultimately liberation, one must practice the following vows in thought, speech, and action:

- **Non-violence:** The fundamental vow from which all other vows stem. It involves minimizing intentional and unintentional harm to any other living creature.
- **Truthfulness:** Practiced in order not to harm others by speech.
- **Non-stealing:** Principle of not taking, or having intentions of taking, what belongs to others.
- **Chastity:** For lay Jains, this means avoiding sexual promiscuity. For monks and nuns, it is complete celibacy.
- **Non-materialism:** By limiting the desire for, and acquisition of, material goods, we can reduce attachments and focus on achieving the ultimate goal of nirvana.

Jain Philosophy

Soul/Body: Jains believe that each living being is an integration of Soul and Body. Soul is an eternal non-material entity, which upon death takes re-birth and continues the cycle of life and death until liberation. Liberation is achieved only after the Soul frees itself of all karmic influences of present and past lives.

Tolerance: This philosophy states that no single perspective on an issue contains the whole truth. Substance, time, place, and the observer's conditions all affect the viewpoint. Any event should be considered from different points of view, resulting in a non-dogmatic approach to the doctrines of other faiths.

Karma: All Souls are equal in their potential for attaining enlightenment and liberation. Different types of Karma, however, limit this ability of the Soul. Karma is understood as a form of subtle matter that adheres to the Soul as a result of its actions of body, speech, and mind. This accumulated Karma is the cause of the Soul's bondage in the cycle of birth and death.

Moksha or Nirvana (eternal liberation through enlightenment): The ultimate aim of life is to liberate the Soul from the cycle of birth and death. This is done by eliminating all bound Karmas and preventing further accumulation. When the Soul progresses to its pure state of omniscient knowledge, free of all Karma, it achieves "Moksha" or "Nirvana."

Path to Liberation: Jains believe in the three-fold path of Right Perception, Right Knowledge and Right Conduct to attain liberation or "Nirvana:"

1. Samyak Darshan (Right Perception): Belief in the body, Soul and Karma relationship as described in Jainism.

2. Samyak Jnän(Right Knowledge): Knowledge of the operation of Karma and its relationship to the Soul.

3. Samyak Charitra (Right Conduct): Adherence to the five vows.

Jain Scriptures

The Jain canon contains either total of 84, 45 or 32 (depending on the tradition) and is divided into three main groups, the Purvas (old texts, 12 books), the Angas (limbs, 12 books) and the Angabahya (subsidiary canon). Many of these scriptures are lost. The Tattvärtha Sutra, written in second century CE, summarizes the entire Jain doctrine and forms the basis for Jain education today.

The Jain Community

The Jain community has contributed enormously to the arts, trade, politics and philosophy of India. Its most visible contribution can be seen in the nation's sculpture and architecture.

There are approximately 7 million Jains in the world, about 100,000 of whom live in North America.

Jainism's Relevance Today

Jain scriptures written more than 2,000 years ago describe in great detail many of the facts that modern science has demonstrated. The vitality of plants, the benefits of drinking filtered/boiled water, the benefits of meditation and yoga, the existence of atoms and molecules, and the benefits of vegetarianism have all been elaborately discussed in Jain scriptures for centuries. In addition, there is much Jain writing about subjects such as physics, mathematics, and astronomy. Furthermore, Jains have been promoting equality for women, animal rights, and environmental awareness.

There are still many hidden treasures within Jainism that the world is just discovering. Specifically, the practice of non-violence, the power of forgiveness, the utility of self-control, reincarnation, environmentalism and the fact that all actions have associated reactions or consequences (Karmas).

"Ahimsa Paramo Dharma – Non-Violence is the greatest Dharma" — Mahävir

Source: Jain Center of Greater Boston

Jain Prayers

Namokar Mantra
Namo Arihantänam **(12 Attributes) –**
I bow to Arihantas

I bow to the Arihantas (Perfect Human Souls) because they have achieved absolute truth and devote themselves to the uplifting of life on earth. These perfect souls have reached enlightenment by overcoming inner enemies and weaknesses, have attained infinite knowledge, infinite bliss, and showed us the path that brings an end to the cycle of birth and death.

Namo Siddhänam **(8 Attributes) –**
I bow to Siddhas

I bow to the Siddhas (Liberated Souls) because they possess infinite perception, knowledge, and bliss. Siddhas have attained the state of perfection and immortality by liberating themselves of all Karmas.

Namo Äyariyänam **(36 Attributes) –**
I bow to Ächäryas

I bow to the Ächäryas (Heads of religious orders) because they have mastered the scriptures and principles of religion.

Namo Uvajjhäyänam **(25 Attributes)–**
I bow to Upädhyäys

I bow to the Upädhyäys (those that are well versed in all Ägams, i.e. scriptures) because they teach the deserving pupils and other followers.

Namo Loe Savva Sähunam **(27 Attributes) –**
I bow to all the Sädhus and Sädhvis (monks)

I bow to all the Sädhus (monks) and Sädhvis (nuns) because they devote their lives to the selfless pursuit of enlightenment for all, follow the five great vows of conduct and inspire us to live a simple Jain Way of Life.

Michchhami Dukkadam

KHAMEMI SAVVE JIVA
I forgive all living beings,

SAVVE JIVA KHAMANTU ME
May all souls forgive me,

MITTI ME SAVVA BHOOESU
I am on friendly terms with all,

VERAM MAJJHAM NA KENVI
I have no animosity toward any other Soul,

MICHCHHAMI DUKKADAM
May all my faults be dissolved.

Khamasaman Sutra

Ichchami I wish
Khamasamano Great Saints
Vandium to bow down
Javanijjae with my best efforts
Nisishiae keeping sinful acts away
Matthen with the head
Vandami I bow down

- Jain Prarthanas, Jain Center of Greater Boston, Mahävir Samvat 2529, March 2003. Complied by Pankaj, Shrenik, and Shardule Shah (audio CD is also available from Jain Center of Greater Boston (www.jcgb.org)
- http://www.jainworld.com/radio/jain_music15.asp – Jain Prayers audio can be found here. Prayers include Navkar Mantra, Bhaktamar Stotra, Parshwanath Stotra, Meri Bhavna (My Aspirations), Barah Bhävanä (12 Reflections), Tattvarth Sutra, English Songs, Gujarati Songs, etc.

My Aspirations
Meri Bhävanä

He who conquered love and hatred,
and vanquished sensual temptation,
True cosmic knowledge who attained
and showed the path to salvation;

Some may call Him Buddha, Hari, Jina,
or may call him Brahma, Supreme;
His thoughts and deep devotion may be
in my heart and mind and dream.

Who do not long for sensual zest,
whose feelings are gentle and right;
In well being of world and self,
who do endeavor day and night.

Who do penance of selflessness and
who have no regrets in life;
To lessen sufferings of this world,
such learned sages do strive.

May I always look up to them and
may I keep them in my mind;
Practice their conduct in my life,
I wish my mind be so inclined.

May I never injure a life; of lying,
may I never think;
Not wanting others' wealth and spouse,
contentment-nectar may I drink.

May egotism I never feel; angry,
may never I become;
On seeing others' worldly wealth,
to envy may I not succumb.

May I always feel and ponder to act
in a true and sincere way;
I always may do good to all,
as far as I can, every day.

For living beings of the world,
feelings of friendship may I show;
For woeful creatures, from my heart,
may stream of kindness ever flow.

The cruel, wicked and evil doers,
my mood and mind may not resent;
May thoughts of mine be so mended,
of others I may be tolerant.

My heart may be so full of love,
whenever I see a noble man;
My mind may be so full of joy,
I serve him as much as I can.

May I never be ungrateful;
malice never be in my mind;
May I not see faults of people;
high virtues may I always find.

Let someone call me good or bad,
let riches come or turn away,
Whether I live for a million years,
or I face death this very day.

Whether someone does frighten me,
or even tempt me in some way;
May my steps never falter from
proven good and righteous way.

Neither may I be too joyous,
nor may I be nervous in pain;
I may not dread a stormy river, jungle,
ghost or rough mountain.

Firm, unshaken and well balanced,
my mind may ever grow and grow;
In beloved's passing, evil's face,
and endurance may I ever show.

May worldly creatures be blissful,
uneasiness may no one feel;
Forgetting ill will, pride and guilt,
new songs of joy may sing with zeal.

May truth be talk of every home,
there be no sign of evil act;
Enlightened people may improve,
fruits of this life may get, in fact.

Misfortune, dread may never come;
bountiful rains come well in time;
May rulers always be righteous,
may justice be even, sublime.

Disease and famine may not be;
may people have plenty and peace;
Nonviolence be the rule of the world,
may the world be full of joy and ease.

May mutual love pervade the world
and dark delusions fade away;
Untrue, unkind, intriguing, harsh,
such words, no one may ever say.

May all become Yugvir at heart;
welfare and peace may all attain;
Facing all sorrows with patience,
nature of truth may all men gain.

"Only that man can take a right decision, whose Soul is not tormented by the afflictions of attachment and aversion."
— Isibhasiyam (44/1)

- Original Author: Pandit Jugal Kishor Mukhtar
- English translation: Devendra Kumar Jain
- http://www.jainworld.com/radio/jain_music4.asp – My Aspirations in Hindi (Meri Bhavna)

Treasures in Jainism
Thousands-of-years-old practices validated by modern science

For more than 2,500 years, Jains have been on a path of Non-Violence, Non-Absolutism (respecting other views), and Non-Possessiveness. Jainism is based on strong scientific principles.

Only recently have scientific advances validated what Jains have been practicing for thousands of years. The following are some of the practices:

Jain Practices and Modern Science

Jain Practices	Validation by Science
Non-Violence – Compassion	The solution to modern day social and political problems. Terrorism can be solved only through comprehensive Non-Violent means.
Vegetarianism	FDA (Food and Drug Adminstration) guidelines now show a food pyramid consisting of a primarily vegetarian diet.
Meditation	Meditation has tremendous therapeutic effects, including altering brain chemistry and physical changes, encouraging feelings of compassion.[1] In some schools children are encouraged to meditate before taking standardized exams.
Yoga	Tremendous benefits in this practice. Yoga is now being taught in high schools, colleges, and in towns and health clubs throughout the nation.
Drinking filtered/boiled water	Hundreds of millions of lives could have been saved in years past if this common Jain practice was universally adopted.
Respecting plants as living beings	Only recently has science accepted that plants are living organisms.

Jain Practices	Validation by Science
Respecting nature	Today, science is discovering that only balanced environmental practices can solve the problems facing the world.
Jain mathematics	The extensive body of Jain literature discusses many concepts in mathematics.
Equality for women	Even today, most of the world is not practicing this. Jains believe that all Souls are equal and have a potential to achieve the highest state.
Forgiveness in thoughts, words and deeds	Science now believes that in this complex and difficult world, forgiveness is the path to happiness. [1]
Animal protection	Jains have formed many institutions for protecting animals of all kinds. Only today is there an effort to protect endangered species.
Molecules and atoms	Tattvarth Sutra and other Jain scriptures mention the existence of Paramanu – the smallest indivisible particle.
Ethics and compliance	Jains are known for their strong business ethics. Corporations and business schools are focusing more on ethics and compliance.
Many viewpoints – Tolerance (Anekantvad)	Current management practices and leaders are succeeding by recognizing that issues are complex and that only by collecting and integrating different views can they make optimal decisions.
Non-Possessiveness	People have realized that consumerism is not the path to happiness. Living in balance with possessions simplifies one's life, as well as promoting the sharing of natural resources with fellow humans and other living beings.
Karma – for every action there is a reaction	This was not evident to societies in the past. But we know today that even thoughts can provoke hormonal changes and alter our actions. We also know violence has a vicious, reactionary nature.

For thousands of years, Jains have been practicing the above beliefs, which modern science and practices are validating. And now more than ever, the Western world can leverage Jain philosophy. Only now is North America and the rest of the world truly discovering what Jains have known. Imagine, if the Jains had shared this treasure with the world sooner, this world would have been a very different place. But it is not too late. When you plant a seed, the soil has to be right, there has to be enough light and water for a great big tree to grow. The environment has to be conducive. In the same way, the North American and Western environment in which we live is conducive to sharing and benefiting from these treasures.

Far from Validation

In addition to the above beliefs and practices, Jainism also believes in the following, which are not part of mainstream science theories but may be validated in the future:

- **Concept of Soul** – Jainism has a distinct concept that each individual has a Soul, and the body is just the housing. Upon death the Soul enters another body.

- **Reincarnation** – The Soul lives on after death and reincarnates into another living being. This cycle continues until the Soul becomes fully realized (perfect) and sheds all the past negative vibrations (Karma).

- **Cosmology** – Jain scriptures have extensive discussions of multiple universes, distances, different worlds, non-human celestial (Devata) and hellish (Naraki) beings.

- **Managing Passions** – A Jain's focus is to manage his or her passions of Anger, Pride, Deceit, and Greed. Only by focusing, understanding and managing these passions can Jains strengthen their practice of non-violence and reduce the negative vibrations on the Soul. The greater the progress of Soul purification, the lower the intensity of these passions.

"Would the system established by ancestors hold true upon examination? If it does not, I am not here to justify it for the sake of saving the traditional grace of the dead, irrespective of the wrath I may have to face."
— Dwatrinshika of Siddhasen Diwarkar

---

[1] "How Thinking Can Change the Brain," *Wall Street Journal*, Jan. 19, 2007
- JAINA Convention 2005, "Introduction to Jainism and Science," by Yogendra Jain
- Extracts from JAINA Vision2020 and Tattvarth Sutra presentation developed by JCGB Level 6 Pathshala and Yogendra Jain

LIVE AND LET LIVE

Non-Violence (Ahimsa)

Ahimsa paramo dharmah – Non-Violence is the supreme religion

The essence of Jainism is Ahimsa (Non-Violence). All Jain beliefs, practices, rituals, and traditions emanate from this central theme. Jains practice Ahimsa not only toward human beings but also toward all living beings. Ancient Jain texts explain that violence (Himsä) is defined by intentional or unintentional harm. It is the intention to harm, the absence of compassion, that makes an action more violent. Without violent thoughts there could be no violent actions.

- Non-Violence is avoiding harm by our actions, our speech, and our thoughts.
- Non-Violence is loving through our actions, our speech, and our thoughts.

The Six-Step Ladder of Non-Violence

The first three steps remind us not to harm anyone; the next three steps remind us to love others. The first step is avoiding harm by our actions, because physically injuring someone is most painful. The second step is not using our speech, things we say, as a means to hurt others. The third step is reducing or eliminating our thoughts of harming or being deceitful toward others, because intentions are often the root cause of what we say and do to others.

The next three steps are that we love others. The fourth step is developing thoughts of compassion and sacrifice for others. The fifth step is talking in a loving manner, like complimenting and praising others. Finally, the sixth step is taking action or doing acts of kindness and selflessness. The Ladder of Non-Violence is an easy way to reflect on what we think, say, and do every day to see if we are being as nonviolent as possible. By taking these steps we can move toward total Non-Violence in our lives.

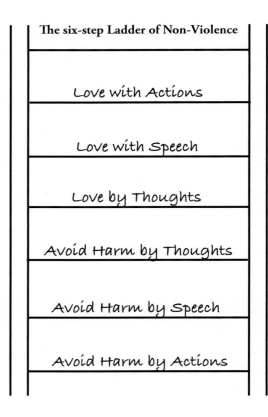

The six-step Ladder of Non-Violence

Love with Actions

Love with Speech

Love by Thoughts

Avoid Harm by Thoughts

Avoid Harm by Speech

Avoid Harm by Actions

Definition of Non-Violence (Ahimsa)

*Mentally, verbally, physically, directly, indirectly,
knowingly, unknowingly,
intentionally, unconditionally
not by self, not through others (engage or ask others) and not
to condone or provide support in any shape or form
TO
injure, harm, abuse, oppress, enslave, insult, discriminate,
torment, persecute, torture, or kill any creature or living
being (humans or non-humans)*

Circle of Non-Violence

Most people agree that it is important to lead a life of Non-Violence, but then the question comes up, "Whom should we be nonviolent toward?"

The Circle of Non-Violence is multi-layered. We begin with being nonviolent toward the self. This means that we do not harm ourselves physically by smoking, drinking, or using illicit drugs. Also, it means that we do not harm ourselves mentally by stress, self criticism, or negative thoughts. From the Self, we expand our circle of Non-Violence toward Family, Friends, and Society. Probably the most difficult practice is compassion and forgiveness toward our Enemies, which is the next circle, and finally Environment.

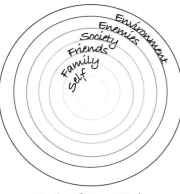

Circle of Non-Violence

Cycle of Violence

Violence is not static, rather it is a dynamic cycle. Violence is infectious. Violence perpetuates further violence just as a stone which is thrown in calm water creates ripples.

Transformation

We must transform our thoughts, speech and actions. Specifically:

Thoughts:
Anger —> Forgiveness
Hatred —> Understanding

Speech:
Gossip —> Praise
Curse —> Compliment

Actions:
Hurting —> Healing
Discrimination —> Practice Equality

Non-Violence is the ultimate transformation necessary to solve all personal, local, and global conflicts, as well as a path for lasting peace and happiness for all.

For monks and nuns as well as spiritually advanced laypeople, the practice of Non-Violence is further enhanced and fortified by the five Mahävratas (Major Vows). The vows are Non-Violence, Truth, Non-Stealing, Celibacy, and Non-Possessiveness.

"Ahimsa Paramo Dharma – Non-Violence is the greatest Dharma." — Mahävir

Source: From Non-Violence booklet by Sapna Jain and Dr. Manoj Jain

Non-Absolutism
(Anekantvad – Multi-faceted Viewpoints)
Respect for, seeking, and acceptance of multiple viewpoints

One of the three core Jain practices is Non-Absolutism (Anekantvad – multi-faceted viewpoints). The perception of truth or reality from an absolute viewpoint poses two major challenges:

1. Conditioned Perception – Our thinking and conditioning is biased through our backgrounds and experiences. Since our perceptions are subject to our own biases, our very instruments of perception affect what we perceive, thus there can be no single truth. Everyone perceives truth differently.[3]

2. Vast Reality – The second challenge is posed by the "reality" itself. The reality comprises innate qualities of substances and elements, and these are in constant flux. With such complexity even the most extraordinary human can only understand a very small facet of the full reality.

Anekantvad – Because of these challenges, Jains practice Anekantvad, which means multi-faceted viewpoints. It is for these reasons that one cannot claim knowledge of absolute truth, and we must strive for Anekantvad (many aspects of reality and our inherent inability to comprehend absolute truth in its entirety).

Syadvad – This leads to the doctrine of Syadvad or relativity, which states that truth is relative to different viewpoints (nayas). What is true from one point of view is open to question from another. Absolute truth cannot be grasped from any particular viewpoint alone because absolute truth is the sum total of all the different viewpoints that make up the universe. Because it is rooted in the doctrines of Anekantvad and Syadvad, Jainism does not look upon the universe from an anthropocentric, ethnocentric or egocentric viewpoint. It takes into account the viewpoints of other species, other communities and nations, and other human beings. Jains encourage dialog and harmony with other faiths.

Are You a Fundamentalist?

– Do you think you, your God, your scripture, or your view possesses the Truth?

– Do you believe that someone possesses the Truth – the answer to everything?

– Do you have a strict single-sided view of the past, present, and future?

The fundamentalists proclaim that their belief is infallible and that only they have the Truth. To reach their objectives, fundamentalists supersede the wishes, trample the views of the majority of the people, and hijack the political process for their objectives, and use any means, including violence or intimidation, to justify their ends.[2]

Path to Anekantvad - Continuum of Views

Stage 1: Absolutist View – We believe that we have the Truth. Example: CEO of a business thinks in absolute terms and his or her team tends to disengage. When views are either black or white, and there is no room for different opinions, this is an Absolutist view.

Stage 2: Tolerant View – We bear with and tolerate others' thoughts and ideas, yet we are arrogant and self-righteous about our own view. We do not take any steps to learn more about others' views.

Stage 3: Dialog View – We take active steps to explore the many perspectives that exist. This may include learning about others' faiths and interacting with new people. Here we take the perspective that "I have a view, yet I wish to explore other's views."

Stage 4: Open-mindedness View – Belief that not only my view or one view is the right view, but rather that there is a collage of views which lead to the Truth. Here, we take the perspective that "I have a view and it may not be the most correct, and I am willing to listen to others' views."

Stage 5: Acceptance View – Acceptance of all perspectives, and a humble respect for differences in beliefs. However, acceptance does not mean agreement with all the views; one can believe in only one faith and still have an accepting view of other faiths. Acceptance is not imposing your views on others, even if you believe your view is closer to Truth.

How Do We Become Open-Minded?

There are three steps to becoming open-minded.

Step 1: Stop and Acknowledge that another view exists

Step 2: Listen to and Learn others' views

Step 3: Accept and Respect all views

The Blind Men and the Elephant

by John Godfrey Saxe

American poet John Godfrey Saxe (1816-1887) based the following poem on a Jain fable which was told in India centuries ago.

It was six men of Indostan
To learning much inclined,
Who went to see the Elephant
(Though all of them were blind),
That each by observation
Might satisfy his mind
The First approached the Elephant,
And happening to fall
Against his broad and sturdy side,
At once began to bawl:
"God bless me! but the Elephant
Is very like a wall!"
The Second, feeling of the tusk,
Cried, "Ho! What have we here
So very round and smooth and sharp?
To me 'tis mighty clear
This wonder of an Elephant
Is very like a spear!"
The Third approached the animal,
And happening to take
The squirming trunk within his hands,
Thus boldly up and spake:
"I see," quoth he, "the Elephant
Is very like a snake!"
The Fourth reached out an eager hand,
And felt about the knee.
"What most this wondrous beast is like
Is mighty plain," quoth he;

"'Tis clear enough the Elephant
Is very like a tree!"
The Fifth, who chanced to touch the ear,
Said: "E'en the blindest man
Can tell what this resembles most;
Deny the fact who can
This marvel of an Elephant
Is very like a fan!"
The Sixth no sooner had begun
About the beast to grope,
Than, seizing on the swinging tail
That fell within his scope,
"I see," quoth he, "the Elephant
Is very like a rope!"
And so these men of Indostan
Disputed loud and long,
Each in his own opinion
Exceeding stiff and strong,
Though each was partly in the right,
And all were in the wrong!

Moral
So oft in theologic wars,
The disputants, I ween,
Rail on in utter ignorance
Of what each other mean,
And prate about an Elephant
Not one of them has seen!

"Advocates of religion often suffer from dogmatism. They may agree that what they have known is not absolute truth, but they insist that what others believe is absolutely wrong." — Ächärya Mahapragyaji

-   Extracts from booklet: Fundamentalism by Dr. Manoj Jain
-   Umang Jain, Presenter, Anekantvad – Young Jains of America, 2006
2   "Jainism and the New Spirituality," Dr. Vastupal Parikh, Peace Publications, Toronto 2002

"I see you've security marked your property."

Non-Possessiveness (Aparigraha)

Balancing our needs and desires, while staying detached from possessions

This is one of the three core practices. It asks for minimizing accumulation of possessions and personal enjoyment. The "wants and desires" must be reduced and kept in check as much as possible in thoughts, words, and actions. With the limited resources on this planet, we must be aware of the consequences of our possessiveness. Unchecked possessiveness can lead to great direct harm to oneself, family, society, and the environment.

Relation to Non-Violence: A person obsessed with hoarding, purchasing and consuming may turn to lying, cheating, stealing, and violence to satisfy this habit.

Relation to Non-Absolutism: A person obsessed with possessiveness may be so blinded in accumulating wealth and material goods that he may not see the pain and suffering others had to endure. Also, due to ignorance, a person may not fully understand the environmental impact, as well as the impact to one's mind, health, and family.

At times from hard work, creativity, intelligence, and sheer luck, or from inheritance, a person may gain significant wealth and other possessions. Under such circumstances a person must be vigilant in managing the wealth in a responsible manner, not only to live a comfortable life but also to share the wealth with religious, social and animal care institutions.

Non-Possessiveness Practice in Daily Life

Stuff – Cars, etc.	Taking good care of one's material possessions but ready to share as needed.
Personal Care Products	Using non-animal products (leather, silk, etc.) and being happy and content with such a choice.
TV, Media, Internet, Games	Minimizing time and avoiding addiction with these time-consuming activities.
Family	Loving and caring for all family members but allowing them their space over time and as new relationships form.
Idea	Letting go and embracing different points of view.
Body	Understanding that body, beauty, intelligence, etc. are temporary and embracing change over time in the body. Also understanding that "my real nature is the Soul."
Knowledge	Sharing knowledge with others, and mentoring and guiding them.
Faith	Deep understanding of one's faith but open to other ideas, discoveries, and facts.
Time	Spending time with family, friends and oneself in a balanced manner.
Eating	Embracing healthy food which may be less tasty and avoiding hoarding and blind eating (For example, try eating to only 75% capacity).
Life	Ready to embrace sickness and aging without anger, passion, and fear. Ready to die without clinging to life.
Wealth	Donate a percentage of wealth for the spiritual benefits and material needs of others. Also, detach from ego when donating.

"Keep the house where it belongs, not in the mind. Keep the money in the bank or in the pocket, not in the mind."
— Sri Sri Ravi Shankar

Unity and Diversity Among Jains

The Jain religion is one of the oldest religions in the world, and was also known as Shraman Dharma (austerity) and Nirgranth (detachment) Dharma. It is not an offshoot of any other religion but is an independent religion recognized by these various names during different time periods. Propounders of Jainism in ancient times were also knows as: [3]

- **Shraman (monk):** One who believes in equality of all living beings, practices Non-Violence, and elevates one's Soul by self-effort.
- **Arhat (worthy of worship):** One who lives a virtuous life.
- **Tirthankar (propagators):** One who originates the spiritual path of liberation and establishes the four fold religious order (monks, nuns, laymen, laywomen) after achieving omniscience. There are 24 Tirthankar in this time era and each Tirthankar revitalizes the Jain order.
- **Arihant (destroyer of passions):** One who destroys his inner enemies like anger, greed, passion, ego, etc.

- **Nirgranth (detached):** One who is detached or free from passions and possessions.
- **Jin (conqueror):** One who has conquered all of his desires.

A follower of a Jin is called a Jain and the religion followed by Jains is called Jainism. The current Jain Order (Sangh) was reestablished by Lord Mahāvir, who was the 24th and last Tirthankar of the current time period.

Jainism has several different traditions. There is very little difference among them and whatever little difference is inconsequential. However, each tradition brings a unique perspective and completes the picture in the true sense of Non-Absolutism (Anekantvad). For this reason, Jains are encouraged to keep their traditions but at the same time also participate in other Jain traditions, respect them, and embrace them to complete the Jain view.

Major Jain Traditions

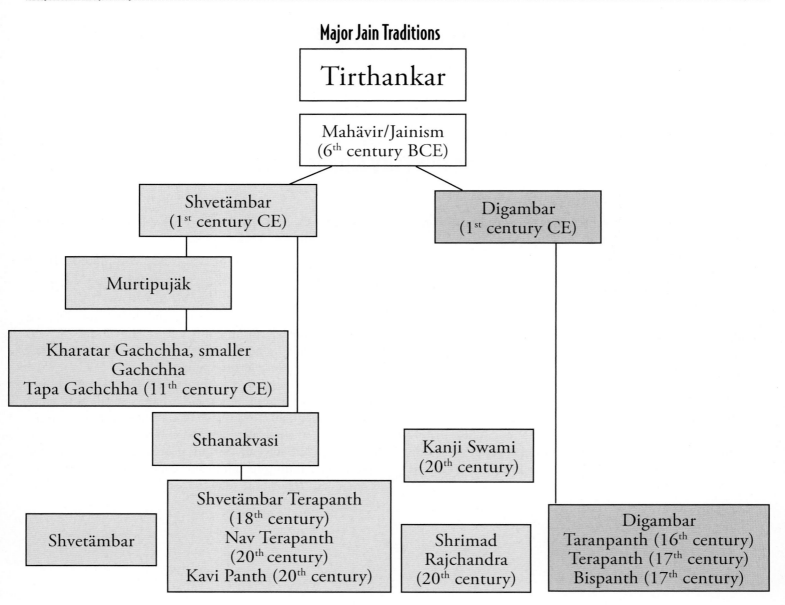

Tirthankar

Mahävir/Jainism
(6th century BCE)

Shvetämbar
(1st century CE)

Digambar
(1st century CE)

Murtipujäk

Kharatar Gachchha, smaller
Gachchha
Tapa Gachchha (11th century CE)

Sthanakvasi

Kanji Swami
(20th century)

Shvetämbar

Shvetämbar Terapanth
(18th century)
Nav Terapanth
(20th century)
Kavi Panth (20th century)

Shrimad
Rajchandra
(20th century)

Digambar
Taranpanth (16th century)
Terapanth (17th century)
Bispanth (17th century)

	Shvetämbar/ Murtipujäk	Digambar	Sthanakvasi	Comment
Idols	Decorated	Not decorated	None	Decorated and undecorated idols are different forms. Decorated is the life of a king that these Tirthankars lived and undecorated form is their life when they achieved total knowledge – keval jnän.
Rituals	Yes	Yes	No	
Ascetics	Wear white clothes	The monks in highest stage do not wear any clothes. Clothes are considered external possessions.	Wear white clothes	
Scriptures	Valabhi Council was held in 5th century and collected the 11 Angas (the 12th one was lost).	Deny the authority of the texts collected by this Council. Claim that 14 Purvas are lost and the last person to know these scriptures died 436 years after Mahävir.	Believe in Shvetämbar scriptures	
Moksha	Men and women can attain Moksha	One has to take birth as a man to attain Moksha as their body makeup allows them to give up all possessions.		All traditions agree that in today's times no one can achieve Moksha, as the general environment for penance does not exist. Hence this is not an issue in this time era.
Mother's Dreams and Embryo	14 dreams; Mahävir's embryo was taken out of the womb of a Brahman woman and transferred to Mother Trishla's. Mahävir was married and had a daughter.	16 dreams; Mahävir's embryo was not transferred; Mahävir did not marry.		Again, these are part of life stories that have been written and rewritten many times, and minor differences and additions have propagated over time.
19th Tirthankar	Malli was a woman	Malli was a man		

Though all the sects mentioned have minor differences in practices, they unanimously accept and believe in Non-Violence, Truthfulness, Non-Stealing, Celibacy, Non-Attachment, Anekantvad, Atma (Soul), Karma and Jain metaphysics.

Jainism is mainly divided into two major sects, namely, Shvetämbar and Digambar. Other splits happened over the years and one prominent split was Sthanakvasi.

Shvetämbar – Murtipujäk (Idol Worshippers)

The Sädhus and Sädhvis of this sect wear white dress. They accept the 45 Ägam granths, and all the Shästras and commentaries written by the great Ächäryas of the past. Worship and spiritual endeavors are equal for both men and women. They worship and decorate the idols.

Shvetämbar – Sthanakvasi

The Sthanakvasi arose as reformers to Shvetämbar Murtipujäk (Idol Worshippers). Lonka Shah, a rich and well read merchant of Ahemdabad, noticed the excesses and misguidance of yatis (temple caretakers who performed rituals). He studied the Jain scriptures and found that idol worship was not included in Jain tenets. Instead he emphasized the study of scriptures (Ägam) and following of Jain path to Soul purification. This was the preamble to the branching of the Sthanakvasi sect which came into being as a non-idol worshippers.

Sthanakvasis do not have temples but have *sthanaks* (prayer halls) where they carry on their religious fasts, festivals, practices, prayers, discourses, etc. Further, the ascetics of Sthanakvasis cover their mouths with strips of cloth. They agree to the authenticity of only 32 of the scriptures of Shvetämbars.

Shvetämbar – Terapanth

This sect arose from Sthanakvasis and was founded by a monk named Swami Bhikhanji in 1760 A.D. Swami Bhikhanji had slight differences in the interpretations of mercy and charity. Like Sthanakavasis, Terraphanthis also do not worship idols and the ascetics use a piece of white cloth to cover their mouth. Ascetics of all Shvetämbar sects use wooden pots for begging for food and water and a soft bristled broom to protect small beings.

Digambars

In Digambar tradition idols are not decorated. The Digambar monks who have reached the highest stages of spiritual state do not wear or keep any clothes. They carry in their hands a Kamandal, a special kind of pot and a broom (Pichchi) made of fallen peacocks' feathers. They eat food once a day with both their palms folded in a shape of a bowl (they do not eat it off a plate, etc.).

Shrimad Rajchandra

This new Jain tradition was inspired by Shrimad Rajchandra. Rajchandra was born in 1867 and died at a young age of 34. He was a child prodigy who had tremendous insight, memory, and past life remembrance. As for his Jain teachings, he was greatly influenced by Ächärya Kundkund, and focused Jains toward inward meditation and self reflection and deemphasized rituals. Rajchandra also had the wisdom to see the root causes of "crippling social customs and quarrels" in society and wrote

> "The more I consider his (Shrimad Rajchandra's) life and his writings, the more I consider him to have been the best Indian of his times. Indeed, I put him much higher than Tolstoy in religious perception." — Mahatma Gandhi

a book on the causes of "Backwardness in Women." Many of Mahatma Gandhi's beliefs and practices came from his friendship with Rajchandra. Gandhi's stance towards equality of women, emancipation of the lower castes, Satyagraha (Truth struggle) were rooted in Rajchandra's guidance.

Reason for the split between Digambar and Shvetämbar

Lord Mahävir's teachings were carried on by his Ganadhars to us in the form of scriptures (Ägams). They were compiled into 12 separate parts, known as the dvadashangi (12 parts). These 12 compositions were acceptable to all followers. However, the Dvadashangi were not written for a long time. The Jain pupils learned them by memorizing them. About 150 years after the nirvana of Lord Mahävir, there was a 12-year drought. During this time, some monks along with Bhadrabahuswami migrated to the South. After the drought was over, some monks came back to the North. They observed that there was some inconsistency in oral recollection of the Jain scriptures, and that the monks that had stayed back relaxed some of their practices, including wearing clothes.

The inconsistencies in the scriptural recollection persuaded them to compile scriptures. To accomplish that, the first council (conference) of monks was held in Patliputra about 160 years after Lord Mahävir's nirvana. Monk Bhadrabahu, who had the knowledge of all 12 Angas, could not be present at that meeting. The rest of the monks could compile only the first eleven Angas by recollection and thus, the twelfth Anga was lost. The monks from the South did not agree with this compilation, and the first split in Jainism started. Jains divided into two main groups, Shvetämbars and Digambas.

"All souls are alike. None is superior or inferior." — Mahävir

Lord Mahävir and His Teachings – Complied by Pravin Shah
www.jainworld.com
"History of Jainism: Digambar – Shvetämbar Insignificant Differences," Jain Study Circular, Dr. Dulichand Jain, 1989
Contributor: Preeti Jain

PEACE

24 Reasons to Believe in and
Live a Jain Way of Life

Practical experience and validation through new scientific discoveries can reinforce our faith in a Jain Way of Life (JWOL).

The following are 24 reasons for you to Live and Share a Jain Way of Life.

JWOL promotes happiness	If I am compassionate toward others around me, they will also be compassionate toward me and my family, my community, and the world will be a much happier place.
Good for children	All parents want their children to thrive in this society while remaining grounded in spirituality and tradition. Jainism and science walk hand in hand. Jain practices guide children toward a way of life which offers practical solutions to day-to-day issues while encouraging deep spiritual reflections on the nature of our Soul.
Good for the mind	Living a life of compassion and meditating on Non-Violence can actually rewire my brain and help me better manage my emotions.[3]
Makes me a leader	Jainism's three core principles are all qualities that great leaders have. Non-Violence allows leaders to be kind to others. Non-Absolutism allows a leader to be open-minded and allows others to share their views. Non-Possessiveness allows the leader to share with others.
Offers a purpose in life	Souls render service to each other (Parasparopagraho Jivanam). Our purpose is to help others. Our purpose is to help ourselves in managing our passions (anger, pride, deceit, and ego).
Promotes conflict resolution	We face many conflicts, not just with people surrounding us but internally in our mind as well. Jainism offers a guide to resolve these issues with compassion and open-mindedness.
Free choice	No elaborate ceremony is needed, no forced conversion takes place, no one forces you to practice it. As I increase my knowledge and faith, I see the value and benefits. I can evolve my conduct to lead a Jain Way of Life.

Encourages the respect of all living beings	Humans, even in our highly evolved times, show utter disregard for other living beings. In fact, many of our religious, research, entertainment, fashion, and dietary practices lead to torturing and killing other animals. We fail to understand that we are just one cog in the ecosystem wheel and that we must respect all living beings.
Promotes ecological balance	With 1.2 billion heads of cattle bred for factory farming, each producing 200-300 liters of methane per day, billions of tons of methane gas are generated. Livestock produce 18% of greenhouse gas emissions as measured in CO_2 equivalent.[4,5]
Reduces chance of cancer	8 out of 10 cancers are dietary-related, and there is a consistently strong correlation between cancer and an animal-based protein diet. Two recent studies of 47,442 men and 88,471 women showed that those eating 5+ servings of bacon each week had 59% greater risk of bladder cancer than those who ate no bacon (52% higher risk for people who ate skinless chicken than those who did not). Even 1.5+ servings of meat daily doubled the risk of cancer.[6,7]
Realistic environmentalism	A "purist environmentalist" is mindful of how his day-to-day actions affect today, as well the future. Jain Way of Life encourages me to minimize violence in thoughts, words, and deeds. It encourages me to take steps to keep the air clean and healthy, consume vegetarian food, respect all forms of life (as they have feelings and are necessary for our survival), and respect all aspects of nature.
Jainism has a long history of Non-Violence	Jain kings, lay people, and priests have not waged wars, killed, tortured, or forcibly converted any other group of individuals. Jains have not only practiced extreme non-violence toward other humans but also they have extended their compassion toward all living beings through the practice of vegetarianism and opening up animal shelters.
Passifistic scriptures	There is no mention of blood, killing, torturing, raping, and other violent acts in Jain scriptures or enacted in ceremonies.
Jainism promotes personal responsibility	In Jainism, God is not responsible for my actions and does not punish or reward. God did not create this world. I am alone responsible for my actions, thoughts, and words. Even if it is someone else's mistake, it is my responsibility to ask for forgiveness and learn from it. I have the will power to manage my emotions, and I can choose to take action which will further escalate the violence of action-reaction, or I can mitigate it by breaking the cycle by taking a compassionate and Non-Violent path.
Self determination	I am responsible for my future. God or an external supernatural force does not control my future.
Healthy vegetarian food	Encourages me to live on a strict vegetarian diet, which is not only compassionate but a healthy diet as well.
Embrace life, embrace death	Death is just changing one body to another and not the end. Soul is immortal. Jainism encourages me to live life to its fullest, and with care and compassion toward all.

Rich rituals and festivals	All walks of life have some rituals. Jainism has many rituals grounded in devotion and practices which are relevant to its philosophy.
Extensive scriptures	Jain scriptures were written 1000s of years ago. They offer systematic, logical, and practical insights of Jain monks, writers, and fully realized individuals (kevalis).
Tolerance	Non-Jain spouses are welcomed in Jain tradition with no requirements of giving up the spouse's previous religious beliefs. In fact, Jainism can coexist with other religious beliefs as long as the core principles of compassion (Non-Violence), respect of other views (Non-Absolutism), and balancing of possessions (Non-Possessiveness) are the foundation in day-to-day life and in raising children.
Balance	Jainism promotes a balanced practice of gaining knowledge (both spiritual and physical), performing rituals, meditating, physical exercise (like yoga), and taking care of family and community.
Forgiveness	At every moment I am encouraged to keep a feeling of forgiveness toward all whom I interact with or whom I inadvertently harm. This helps my mind keep equanimity and peace.
Simplicity	Jainism is simple. Jainism is a religion and a way of life which helps me manage my passions (anger, pride, deceit, ego) through practice of three core beliefs of Non-Violence, Non-Absolutism, and Non-Possessiveness.
Progressive	Embraces scientific principles such as evolution and new theories of universe and mind. As more progress is made in our physical world, we gain an even better understanding of our spiritual world.

"Jain religion is not blind faith. Nor it is emotional worship inspired by fear or wonder.
It is the intuition of the inherent purity of the consciousness will and bliss of the self." — Dr. Nathmal Tatia

3   *The Wall Street Journal*, January 19, 2007, "How Thinking Can Change Your Brain"
4   http://www.cbc.ca/news/background/kyoto/ewe.html – "Ewe, too, can cut greenhouse gases"
5   http://www.fao.org/newsroom/en/news/2006/1000448/index.html
6   http://www.ecomall.com/greenshopping/veggiediet.htm
7   http://www.thecrimson.com/article.aspx?ref=516037
-   http://www.un.org/apps/news/story.asp?NewsID=20772&Cr=global&Cr1=environment#

Vegetarian Way of Life

The word "vegetarian" is derived from the latin word "begetare" that means "to enliven."

Jain philosophy and its practice of Non-Violence and vegetarianism was a positive influence to many non-Jains in ancient India for whom animal consumption and sacrifices were common practices. However, the need for a vegetarian lifestyle is even more applicable today where billions of animals are painfully raised, dismembered, tortured, and slaughtered for food, leather, and other byproducts. Although factory farming is a science in North America, the developing countries are now following America's meat production technology to significantly increase their production levels to meet the demand. Meat eating on a daily basis has become a worldwide epidemic inflicting great suffering on animals.

Very few people see the true picture on how meat reaches their dinner table. Peter Singer tells his experience, "I discovered animal rights in 1978, when I first entered a slaughterhouse and witnessed the violent deaths of terrified dairy cows, pigs, and chickens. What I saw changed my life." All proceeds from this book are donated.

What is Your Vegan Lifestyle?

Jains traditionally have been vegetarians but not vegans. In India as recently as up to 10 years ago, even in big cities, most of the milk production came from farmers who raised their cows on farms, milked them twice a day, left ample milk for the calf, and let them graze in fields. Hence the vegan practice was not necessary. As the dairy industry was mechanized and pain, suffering, and killing of dairy cows became common practice, some Jains are transforming to consuming organic dairy products and embracing a vegan lifestyle. However, even organic dairy products cause violence, and by only a slightly lesser degree than non-organic. Due to economic reasons, even small dairy farmers sell unproductive cows which end up in slaughterhouses.

Type of Vegetarians

Fruitarians	Eat fruit, fruit-like vegetables, and some nuts and seeds
Raw/Living Foodist	Eat only raw food as enzymes are destroyed by cooking
Vegan	Eat no animal products including dairy products (eggs, milk, honey, etc.)
Lacto	Eat dairy but not eggs, gelatin, rennet, etc.
Lacto-ovo	Consume dairy products including eggs

Vegetarians in North America as well as worldwide are increasing. All major cities and colleges have vegetarian clubs. There are many books and 1000s of web sites devoted to this. In addition to living a life of Non-Violence and compassion, there are health, economic, and environmental reasons to embrace a vegetarian lifestyle.

Reasons to be a Vegetarian

Non-Violence	Live and Let Live. Living a compassionate lifestyle we can become truly well rounded in our practice and achieve balance, peace, and harmony with our surroundings.
Physical Health	Obesity, cancer, heart disease and many other ailments are attributed to consumption of meat.
Spiritual Health	Many traditions require a vegetarian lifestyle for their monks, nuns, and spiritual aspirants.
Economic	There is tremendous economic waste of precious resources (water, air, land, and opportunity cost) in meat production.
Slaughtering	Although United States and Canada have laws for humane slaughter, the practice on the meat factory floor is quite different. In fact many worker injuries take place due to the fast paced mechanized slaughter.

Water	– Water Consumption – Slaughtering animals requires hundreds of millions of gallons of water every day. 2 billion tons of waste ends up in waterways, polluting and killing thousands of fish and creating a human health problem. – Livestock production accounts for more than half of all the water consumed in the United States.
Air	World's 1.3 billion cows annually produce 100 million tons of methane, a powerful greenhouse gas which traps 25 times as much solar heat as CO_2.
Land	- Half of American croplands grow livestock feed for meat and dairy products. - 2% of U.S. cropland produces fruits and vegetables while 64% of U.S. cropland is producing livestock feed. - One acre of prime land can make 5,000 lb. of cherries, 10,000 lbs. of green beans, 30,000 lbs. of carrots, 40,000 lbs. of potatoes, 50,000 lbs. of tomatoes, but only 250 lbs. of beef. - 220 million acres of land in the United States have been deforested for livestock production. - 85% of annual U.S. topsoil loss is directly associated with raising livestock.

Religion

No faiths or religious traditions force a meat diet. In fact the scriptures such as the Bible, the Koran, and the Bhagvad Gita encourage their aspirants to live with respect for all living beings.

Vegetarianism in Other Faiths and Civilization

Christian	The Bible states "And God said, 'Behold, I've given you every herb-bearing seed, which is upon the face of the earth, and every tree in which are fruits; for you it shall be meat.'" "Thou shalt not kill."
Islam	The Holy Prophet Muhammad (S) was asked by his companions if kindness to animals was rewarded in the life hereafter. He replied "Yes, there is a meritorious reward for kindness to every living creature." (Bukhari) All creatures on earth are sentient beings. "There is not an animal on earth, nor a bird that flies on its wings – but they are communities like you." (The Quran, 6:38)
Hinduism	Meat can never be obtained without injury to living creatures, and injury to sentient beings is detrimental to (the attainment of) heavenly bliss; let him therefore shun (the use of) meat (Manusmriti, 5:48) 20-30% of Hindus are vegetarians.
Judaism	"And God said: 'Behold I have given you every herb yielding seed which is upon the face of the earth, and every tree, in which is the fruit of a tree yielding seed – to you it shall be for food.'"(Genesis 1:29)
Buddhism	"As the flesh is formed from the blood and sperm, so it is not eatable by the follower of Buddhism, who wishes to have purity." "The eating of meat extinguishes the seed of great compassion." -The Buddha, Mahaparinirvana Sutra
Early Greeks, Egyptians, Hebrews	Many were fruit eaters. Plato, Socrates, and Pythagoras supported a vegetarian diet.

Slaughtered per day in the United States
Cattle – 130,000
Calves – 7,000
Hogs – 360,000
Chickens – 24,000,000

Animal Abuse in Our World

Animal Abuse	In the United States
Slaughtered for Food	Cattle – 130,000 slaughtered per day Calves – 7,000 slaughtered per day Hogs – 360,000 slaughtered per day Chickens – 24,000,000 slaughtered per day
Abuse of Cattle for Meat	Slaughtering of 70% to 80% of baby calves within six months by veal industry or within five years by the beef industry. Slaughtering of the mother cows after five years of their fertile life (life expectancy is 15 years).
Abuse of Cattle for Milk	Cows are kept pregnant continually. Everyday hormones or drugs are injected to increase milk yield. Unproductive cows and calves are slaughtered.

If Americans reduced their meat/dairy intake by just 10%, the savings in grains and soybeans could feed 60 million people per year worldwide. About 24,000 people die every day from hunger or hunger-related causes. Three-fourths of the deaths are children under the age of five. The following are additional statistics on the cost and impact of meat eating:

- The cost of raw materials consumed to produce food from livestock is greater than the value of all oil, gas and coal consumed in America.

- Growing grains, vegetables and fruits uses less than 5% as much raw materials as does meat and dairy production.

- 2 calories of fossil fuel is used for 1 calorie of protein of soybeans, while 78 calories of fossil fuel is used for 1 calorie of beef.

- 6.9 kg of grain and soy makes 1 kg of boneless trimmed pork.

Chickens	These animals are intelligent, inquisitive, nurturing, social beings. They are raised in filthy conditions with thousands of other birds and with cages stacked such that the excrement from the cage above flows down on top of other birds. They are drugged, fattened and many eventually develop premature and painful organ failure, heart attacks, and crippled legs. Their beaks (which are highly sensitive) are cut so they will not peck each other. Over 100 million male chicks (not bread for meat) are ground up alive. Many are thrown in hot water to remove their feathers. Chickens do not have federal legal protection (not exempt from Humane Methods of Slaughter Act).
Cows	Just like human mothers, cows have strong maternal bonds. They cry for days when separated from their babies. They are burned with hot iron (branded), castrated (testicals are ripped out), given massive amounts of hormones for gaining weight, and transported long distances in tiny holders for slaughter. Some meet their end by a bolt gun shot through their head. However, some still remain conscious and are dismembered alive.

Pigs	They are sensitive, warm, playful, and intelligent. Some have their teeth cut off, testicals ripped out, and tails cut. Breeding sows are constantly impregnated. 1 million pigs die in transport and another 360,000 are crippled by the time they arrive at the slaughterhouse every year.
Fish	More than 30% of sea animals consumed are raised on a farm. It takes a great amount of resources to raise a fish. It takes five pounds of wild caught fish to produce 1 pound of farmed fish.
Turkeys	These are agile and beautiful creatures which can fly 55 miles an hour and run 25 miles per hour. Factory raised turkeys live only 5-6 months.
Ducks and Geese	Many are raised for foie gras – a delicacy. Two pounds of grain are pumped down their throats and into the stomach to produce a diseased "fatty liver" which is foie gras. The state of California has banned foie gras.

"Our practice of rearing and killing other animals in order to eat them is a clear instance of the sacrifice of the most important interest of other beings in order to satisfy trivial interest of our own." —Tom Regan (author of The Case for Animal Rights)

Writer: Preeti Jain
- http://www.ivu.org/religion/articles/judaism.html
- http://www.theveggietable.com/articles/whatisavegetarian.html
- http://goveg.com/factoryFarming_chickens.asp

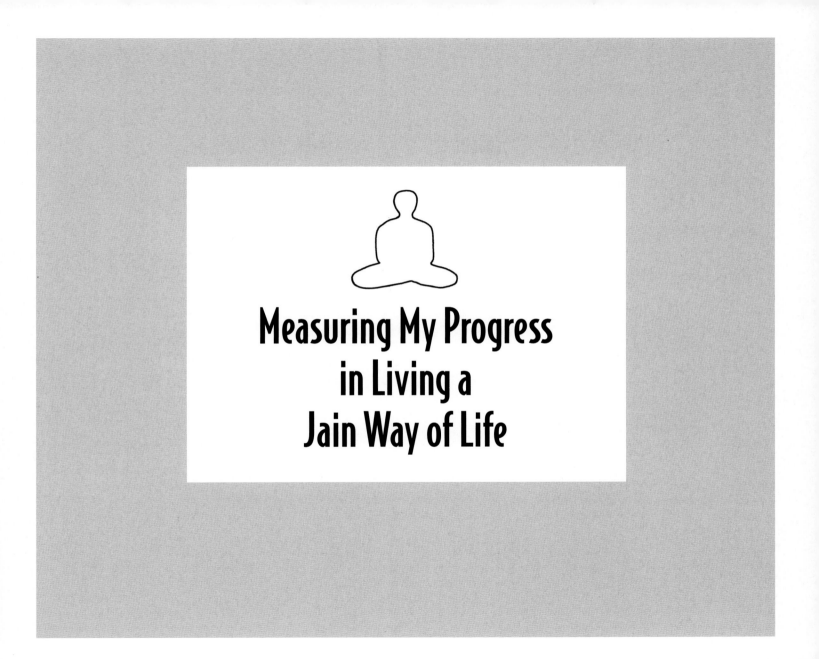

Measuring My Progress in Living a Jain Way of Life

My Mind & My Body
Jain Way of Life – A Self Evaluation

Managing my mind and body is critical for happiness, challenge, discovery, and spiritual growth. JWOL is living a life grounded in thoughts, words, and actions of the core Jain principles of:

- **Non-Violence:** in our diet, speech, and thoughts.
- **Non-Possessiveness:** where we balance our possessions and desire for them.

- **Non-Absolutism:** where we strive to keep our mind open and understand other views.

By taking this simple self-evaluation test you can determine your JWOL state of mind and practice. This exercise will expand your awareness and stimulate your mind in thinking about ways to live and promote a Jain Way of Life. The goal is to progress toward Level 4 and 5.

JWOL mission is to progress toward levels 4 and 5. What level are you on?

	Forgiveness
1	I think cruel thoughts towards people, objects, and situations.
2	I express ill thoughts and keep grudges for years.
3	I mentally forgive a person I despised, or had a disagreement with, and would ask for forgiveness.
4	I ask for forgiveness from a person I've despised, or had a strong disagreement with.
5	I forgive all people and ask for forgiveness from all living beings every moment.

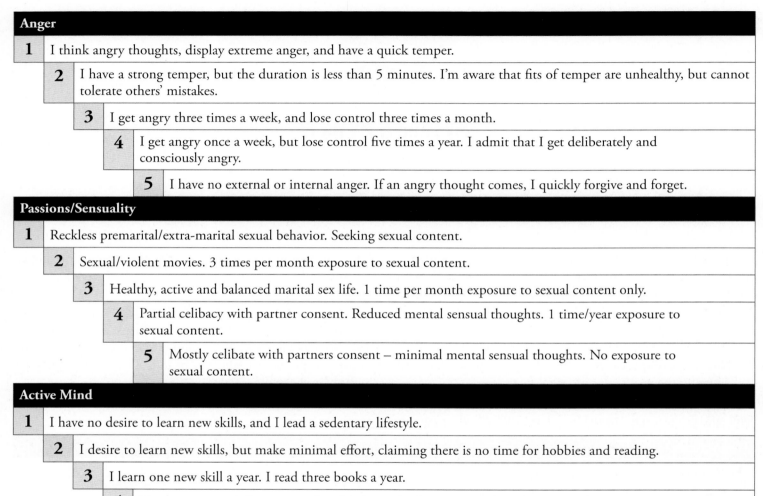

Anger

1	I think angry thoughts, display extreme anger, and have a quick temper.
2	I have a strong temper, but the duration is less than 5 minutes. I'm aware that fits of temper are unhealthy, but cannot tolerate others' mistakes.
3	I get angry three times a week, and lose control three times a month.
4	I get angry once a week, but lose control five times a year. I admit that I get deliberately and consciously angry.
5	I have no external or internal anger. If an angry thought comes, I quickly forgive and forget.

Passions/Sensuality

1	Reckless premarital/extra-marital sexual behavior. Seeking sexual content.
2	Sexual/violent movies. 3 times per month exposure to sexual content.
3	Healthy, active and balanced marital sex life. 1 time per month exposure to sexual content only.
4	Partial celibacy with partner consent. Reduced mental sensual thoughts. 1 time/year exposure to sexual content.
5	Mostly celibate with partners consent – minimal mental sensual thoughts. No exposure to sexual content.

Active Mind

1	I have no desire to learn new skills, and I lead a sedentary lifestyle.
2	I desire to learn new skills, but make minimal effort, claiming there is no time for hobbies and reading.
3	I learn one new skill a year. I read three books a year.
4	I learn one new skill a year, read six books a year, keep a journal, and mentor others.
5	I learn two new skills a year, read ten books, and write extensively, in addition to teaching and lecturing.

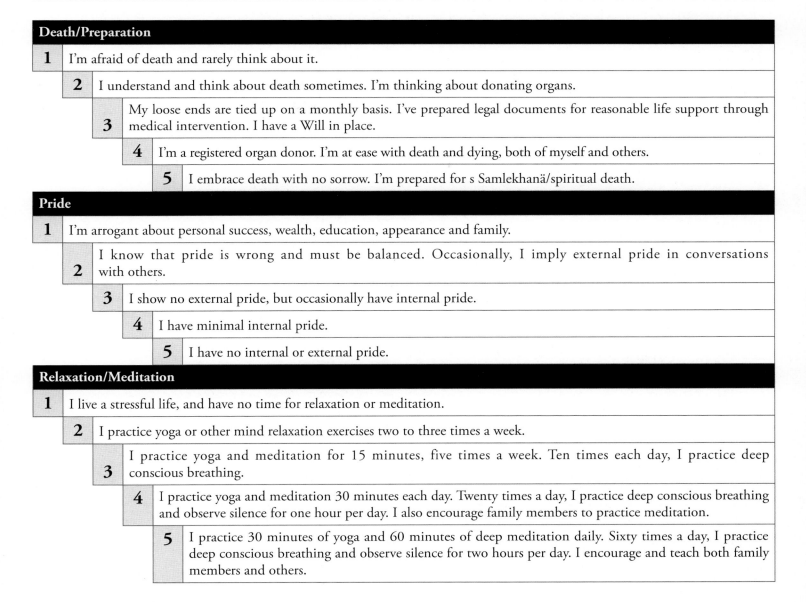

Death/Preparation

| 1 | I'm afraid of death and rarely think about it. |

| | 2 | I understand and think about death sometimes. I'm thinking about donating organs. |

| | | 3 | My loose ends are tied up on a monthly basis. I've prepared legal documents for reasonable life support through medical intervention. I have a Will in place. |

| | | | 4 | I'm a registered organ donor. I'm at ease with death and dying, both of myself and others. |

| | | | | 5 | I embrace death with no sorrow. I'm prepared for s Samlekhanä/spiritual death. |

Pride

| 1 | I'm arrogant about personal success, wealth, education, appearance and family. |

| | 2 | I know that pride is wrong and must be balanced. Occasionally, I imply external pride in conversations with others. |

| | | 3 | I show no external pride, but occasionally have internal pride. |

| | | | 4 | I have minimal internal pride. |

| | | | | 5 | I have no internal or external pride. |

Relaxation/Meditation

| 1 | I live a stressful life, and have no time for relaxation or meditation. |

| | 2 | I practice yoga or other mind relaxation exercises two to three times a week. |

| | | 3 | I practice yoga and meditation for 15 minutes, five times a week. Ten times each day, I practice deep conscious breathing. |

| | | | 4 | I practice yoga and meditation 30 minutes each day. Twenty times a day, I practice deep conscious breathing and observe silence for one hour per day. I also encourage family members to practice meditation. |

| | | | | 5 | I practice 30 minutes of yoga and 60 minutes of deep meditation daily. Sixty times a day, I practice deep conscious breathing and observe silence for two hours per day. I encourage and teach both family members and others. |

Body Care	
1	I have no interest in physical exercise, but enjoy dangerous activities which can harm the body.
2	I walk 3 times a week or play sports twice a week. I have respect for the body.
3	I engage in a cardio exercise/muscle toning program, or play sports three times per week. I get a regular medical checkup.
4	I engage in a cardio exercise/muscle toning program, or play sports four times per week.
5	I engage daily in whole body exercise, yoga, deep breathing, and mindful care of the body.

Vibrations/Karma	
1	What are you talking about?
2	I'm passively aware of the effects of my words and actions, but continue to use words and actions which have negative effects on myself and others.
3	I am very aware of the effect constant mindfulness has on the Karma vibrations of myself and others.
4	I am aware of the ripple effects of Karma vibrations on myself and others.
5	I have a strong awareness of the ripple effects of Karma vibrations on myself, others and the environment.

> *"When the mind becomes stable like the water of a clear pond, then the reflection of the Soul can be seen in it."* — Tattva Sar 41

- Developed by: Pathshala Level 5/6; Jain Center of Greater Boston (JCGB)– Project Members: Students of JCGB Level 5B/6 (Tarang Gosalia, Amit Jain, Monica Jain, Priyanka Jain, Nimit Mehta, Neel Vora, Nirav Shah and support from other members)
- Coordinators: Yogendra Jain, Prakash Teli, Vijay Savla.
- www.yjindia/jwolcalc.asp

My Things

Jain Way of Life – A Self Evaluation

So much of our lives is consumed by collecting, managing, and maintaining "My Things." Some are, of course, necessary for a comfortable lifestyle. However, others distract us and consume tremendous time and energy.

By taking this simple self-evaluation test you can determine your JWOL state of mind and practice. This exercise will expand your awareness and stimulate your mind in thinking about ways to live and share a Jain Way of Life.

Your JWOL mission is to progress toward levels 4 and 5 – What level are you on?

Greed	
1	I'm obsessed with getting a bigger house and car, and I want more money. I'm very jealous of friends and family.
2	I desire a better and bigger house, car, or more money. I'm jealous of friends and family.
3	Occasionally, I desire more comfort and have mild jealousy toward others.
4	I have minimal internal greed, no enviousness of others and I appreciate the things I do have.
5	I am in constant equanimity and balance.

Money

1		I'm obsessed with money. I work day and night and make minimal donations to charities.
	2	I spend a great deal of time managing money. I'm stingy, and donate less than 1% of my income.
	3	I have strong financial planning for my family's well being. I donate 1% to local and 1% to national charitable organizations.
	4	I've vowed to limit my total amount of assets. I donate 4% of my income. I make public donations only to encourage others as I don't desire name recognition.
	5	I make anonymous donations, proactively donating up to 10% or 20% of my income or excess money.

Material Possessions

1		I'm recklessly purchasing clothes, shoes, and jewelry. I tend to hoard things and make impulse buys.
	2	I'm not ready to share my stuff.
	3	I'm internally and externally ready to share my stuff. I let people use my things if needed.
	4	I've vowed to limit my number of shoes to 10 pairs, my clothes to 20 outfits, and to limit purchases.
	5	I make minimal purchases only when needed. I hold simple celebrations. There is minimal clutter in my home.

Travel

1		I do not go on any spiritual retreats, but only travel for pleasure and gambling.
	2	I have a one day retreat once a year. I visit two new spiritual places a year and observe a gambling limit of $100/year.
	3	I have 2 retreats a year, visit four out-of-town spiritual places a year and I appreciate culture, traditions, and nature.
	4	I have three retreats a year, and visit five out-of-town spiritual places a year. I regularly visit an ashram, temple, or church. I do not gamble.
	5	I have 30 total days of retreats a year, and visit 10 spiritual places a year.

"External renunciation is meaningless if the Soul remains fettered by internal shackles." — Bhava-pahuda (13)

My Consumptions

Jain Way of Life – A Self Evaluation

We are physically and mentally consuming. We eat, and think about eating, numerous times a day. We take care of our bodies using many products.

By taking this simple self-evaluation test you can determine your JWOL state of mind and practice of your consumption habits. This exercise will expand your awareness and stimulate your mind in thinking about ways to live and promote a Jain Way of Life.

JWOL mission is to progress toward levels 4 and 5. What level are you on?

Food
1 I'm mostly vegetarian for health reasons. I'm unaware of the source of meat products and their production process.
2 I'm vegetarian, but eat eggs, honey, etc. I'm also careless about checking ingredients.
3 I'm a strict vegetarian. I always check the ingredients of food and drinks, and eat no eggs or honey.
4 I have reduced my dairy intake (a vegan diet) by 75% and root vegetable consumption by 75%.
5 I have a balanced vegan diet. Three times a week I eat only in daytime and avoid root vegetables. I eat out in mostly vegetarian restaurants.

Drinks

1 I drink excessive soda and/or caffeine. I'm a social drinker.

2 I drink soda/caffeine five times a day. I only drink socially once in a while.

3 I have some soda or caffeine about three times a day, but completely abstain from alcohol.

4 I only have soda or caffeine once a day, I avoid sugary drinks, and carrot/root derived vegetarian juices.

5 I only drink filtered water, fresh juices, and soy milk.

Personal/Care Products

1 I'm ignorant of the use of leather, silk, and animal tested products.

2 I'm aware of and prefer a non-animal based solution, but will not go out of the way to get it.

3 I purchase some non-cruelty based products but I have no leather seats in my car and my shoes, purse, belts are all leather free. I have not purchased any new silk clothes.

4 I will only use non-cruelty based products and actively promote these ideas with my friends and family.

5 I've vowed not to purchase animal based products. I actively campaign world wide against animal testing.

Nutrition

1 I have excessive oily, fatty, heavy sugar foods in my diet. I almost never eat fruits.

2 I'm aware of the need for eating a nutritious, balanced diet, but don't follow through.

3 I minimize oily, fatty foods, have one salad a day, and drink four glasses of water a day.

4 I only eat sweets twice a week, and I avoid adding salt while eating.

5 I follow the vegetarian food pyramid. I only eat sweets once a week.

Eating	
1	I'm gluttonous and get upset if my meals are delayed.
2	I overeat, I'm obsessed with spice and flavor, and I'm picky. Also, I eat much too quickly.
3	I don't overeat. I only eat for the sustenance of my body, though I do savor tastes. I'm not finicky. I observe one full-day fast a year, and eat only one meal a day three times a year.
4	I observe three full-day fasts a year, and five days a year I eat only once. I do not eat at night (after sunset) four times a week.
5	I observe 12 full-day fasts a year, 24 one-meal days a year, and refrain from food at night.

"I am not Rama. I have no desire for material things. Like Jin I want to establish peace within myself."
—Yoga Vasishta, Chapter 15, Sloka 8 the saying of Rama

My Life & My World

Jain Way of Life – A Self Evaluation

We are not alone. My Life & My World are part of an ecosystem with tremendous opportunities as well as distractions.

By taking this simple self-evaluation test you can determine your JWOL state of My Life & My World. This exercise will expand your awareness and stimulate your mind in thinking about ways to live and promote a Jain Way of Life.

JWOL mission is to progress toward levels 4 and 5. What level are you on?

	Family/Friends
1	My friends behave badly, have bad habits, and are disrespectful.
2	I criticize my friends and family behind their backs. My celebration of birthdays, anniversaries, etc. has no spiritual context.
3	My focus is my own family. Celebrations have a spiritual context.
4	I help friends and extended family members, both emotionally and financially.
5	I balance spiritual growth with family and social obligations.

Entertainment (Media/Radio/TV/Music/Internet)

1	20+ hours a week of TV, movies, and video games.
2	15+ hours a week of media, mostly for entertainment, some educational, or for self-development.
3	Less than 10 hrs a week of educational media only. I listen to an hour of devotional music a week.
4	Less than 5 hours a week of PG-13 entertainment and 4 hours a week educational or spiritual media.
5	Less than 3 hours a week of entertainment and 5-6 hours of educational or spiritual media.

Animal Compassion and Care

1	I'm unaware of the many types of animal cruelty caused by humans.
2	I'm aware of the animal cruelty problem but take no action to prevent it.
3	I donate 0.1% income toward animal protection and volunteer once a year. I try to make people aware of the problem.
4	I donate 0.3% income and volunteer twice a year. I actively support animal rights.
5	Actively working with organization 5 days/year, donate 0.5% income. Planning to donate 5% of my assets.

Profession/Work

1	I'm critical of others at work, even though my own work lacks luster, and I tend to cheat.
2	I avoid work which directly creates, sells, or promotes violent and/or sensual products; I tend to exaggerate my accomplishments and performance.
3	I have a strong spirit of collaboration and team work.
4	I mentor others, listen to my colleagues and conduct my business with care and compassion.
5	Both my work and family life are strong and balanced. I do non-profit work regularly.

Social Service

1	I have no awareness of social problems, either locally or globally.
2	I sponsor a child in a third world country and donate old clothes and canned food.
3	I sponsor two children and volunteer ten hours a year for social service.
4	I volunteer two hours a week in my community.
5	I volunteer ten hours a week in my community.

Other Living Beings

1	I'll swat an insect and put poison food or inhumane traps out for rats, etc.
2	Insects disgust me and I'm careless in removing them. I'm rough and thoughtless with plants.
3	I respect insects as living beings and carefully remove them. I ask for forgiveness when traveling in cars, planes, trains, etc.
4	I gently shoo away or remove insects with extreme care. I take measures to minimize harm to insects.
5	I look down while walking so as not to step on insects and avoid walking on grass.

Environment

1	I don't recycle, I waste water, food and electricity, and I don't care about any dangers posed to the Earth.
2	My car is a gas guzzler, though I recycle a small portion of my garbage. I waste food, paper products, and take excessively long showers.
3	I actively recycle 80% of my garbage. I carpool, take short showers and have a aware of environmental issues.
4	I'm vigilant about my use of my car, water, and electricity. I use public transportation as often as possible, and avoid wasting food. I try to use non-harmful sources of energy.
5	I mostly use public transportation. I have strong awareness of environmental issues.

"If a man can control his body and mind and thereby refrains from eating animal flesh and wearing animal products, I say he will really be liberated." —The Buddha, From the Surangama Sutra

My Spirituality

Jain Way of Life – A Self Evaluation

There are many distractions on the spiritual path. By taking this simple self-evaluation test you can determine your JWOL state of Spirituality. This exercise will expand your awareness and stimulate your mind in thinking about ways to live and promote a Jain Way of Life.

JWOL mission is to progress toward levels 4 and 5. What level are you on?

Multiple Views (Anekantvad)	
1	Forcing one's view. Not taking the time to understand other views.
2	Understand that there are many views but no active attempt to engage and understand.
3	Soliciting and acting on multiple views. Willing to change one's mind.
4	Pro-actively listening, understanding and correlating different positions.
5	Observing and analyzing from many views with deep insight.

Knowledge

1	I'm not interested in reading, writing or learning about the physical and metaphysical.

	2	I try to understand new developments in science, psychology, technology, sociology, politics, etc. I'm learning about religion.

		3	I think about new developments and discuss them with other people. I compare my beliefs with other people's beliefs and look for similarities.

			4	I readily accept new developments once they have been proven.

				5	I use knowledge purely for physical and spiritual development and upliftment.

Faith, Religion and Scriptures

1	I have no interest in my own or other religions, minimal exposure to scriptures or blind faith in what is written in scriptures.

	2	I'm dogmatic about my religion and/or beliefs, and insist that they are always right. I focus on converting others to my religion. I will discard and ignore evidence and proof if it is contradicting my faith.

		3	I have a strong knowledge of my religion and its strengths and shortcomings. I attempt to understand other faiths, and have some exposure to the scriptures of other faiths. I think critically about meaning and relevancy.

			4	I'm not dogmatic about my faith. I embrace thoughtful change and understand the core philosophies of other faiths. I'm comfortable with conducting research and formulating my own conclusions from it.

				5	I'm very familiar with my own and other faiths. I'm able to incorporate the strong points of all faiths with my own practices and beliefs. I'm well read in other philosophies and very well read in my own, with full clarity on the core essence and meaning.

	Traditions/Celebrations
1	I do not practice traditional or religious holidays.
2	I'm aware of holidays, but don't go out of the way to celebrate them.
3	I celebrate some holidays at home. I'm aware of the holidays of other faiths and the meanings behind them. I celebrate life events (birthdays, anniversaries, marriages, etc.) with a spiritual awareness.
4	I celebrate holidays with passion. I have a strong awareness of the meaning behind the tradition, and enjoy explaining this meaning to others and children.
5	I use holidays for inner meditation, self awareness, and family gatherings.

	Prayers
1	I don't know any prayers or the benefits of prayers.
2	I pray one minute per day and understand the benefits.
3	I pray five minutes per day with devotion and awareness of the meaning and the metaphors. I say a simple prayer before eating meals.
4	I pray 10 minutes per day and before each meal. I go to a temple or a spiritual place once a week.
5	I pray and meditate 30 minutes a day and understand the practice deeply.

To measure your progress online, go to www.yjindia.jwolcal.asp

"Religion without science is blind; Science without religion is lame." — Albert Einstein

Many Dimensions of Violence (Himsa)

Many faces to Himsa (Violence) are hidden behind attractive packaging, marketing campaigns, and special interest groups, including corporations. Media and entertainment (TV, internet, magazines, games, etc.) barrage us with overt and covert violent content and call on us to internalize and propagate these messages. It is up to us to be vigilant and protect our family and community from this onslaught. Furthermore, we must be mindful of how our actions, thoughts, and speech additionally contribute to the cycle of violence.

There are many dimensions to Himsa. In practice, this applies to our food, clothing, furnishings, medicines, sports, entertainment, environment, gender, race and interpersonal relations, business, investments, profession, and different and divergent faiths, traditions, viewpoints, and practices. The following are the many dimensions of Himsa.

Classifications of Himsa in Jain Scriptures

Swaroopi Himsa	is unavoidable for basic life functions such as breathing, speaking, eating, sleeping, walking.
Uddyogi/ Arambhi Himsa	for ethical business purposes to earn a living. Here one must look at the alternatives. Also one must exercise a limit and control on one's needs and wants (Non-Possessiveness, Aparigraha).
Virodhi Himsa	for the defense of the culture, country, and community. Here one must do his/her duty without Raag (attachment), Dwesh (hatred, jealousy, malice), and self interests and gains. This Himsa is acceptable but does bind some Karmas.
Sankalpi Himsa	is premeditated, planned and executed with the full force of mind, speech and body by self and by others. This cannot be condoned under any circumstances. This binds the strongest form of Karmas.

Dimensions of Violence

Personal Bodily Needs	Food, drinks, clothing, beauty, hygiene, footwear, firearms, and medicine.
Furnishings	Leather furniture, fur, down, silk, stuffed animals, ivory, animal horns, etc. for home, auto, and boat. Many of these products are derived from animals, child labor and sweat shops.
Entertainment and Sports	Movies, video games, sports (hockey, boxing, wrestling), toys, games, hunting, shooting, fishing, cock fights, bull fights, horse/dog racing, jokes, ethnic and cultural slurs and insults.
Environment and Ecology	Toxic pollution and waste, chemicals, industrial discharges, hazardous waste dumping, landfills, strip mining, nuclear wastes, bio and medical wastes, deforestation.
Transportation of Goods and People	Killing or torturing of animals, exhaustion and torture due to excess loading, lack of food, water, shelter, rest, and exposure to extreme heat and cold.
Worship and Rituals	Killing, torturing, stoning of animals and humans. Practice of traditions and systems which endanger human and environmental safety.
Practice of Profession and Trade	Disregard of moral and social ethics. Trade, killing, torture and misuse of animals, fish and humans. Practices that directly and indirectly kill or torture humans and animals through engineering, technology, business, law, medicine, accounting, advertising, trading, etc. Use of pesticides and herbicides, dairy farming, etc.
Research, Education, Product Development	Vivisection, product testing and medical research on animals. Dissection in schools.
Justice, Administration, and Governance	Discrimination, racial profiling, unjust and discriminatory laws and regulations, slavery, untouchability, crimes, terrorism, and waging unjust wars.
Investments	Investments and profiting from use of animals and humans, violent media, irresponsible corporations which damage environment and human health and safety.
Conflicts, Litigations, Riots, Wars	Terrorism, personal and family life, religious intolerance, ownership of other's resources, land, and property, discrimination at work and in society based on sex, gender, color of skin, ethnicity, religion, beliefs, traditions, customs, dress, and disability.
Justice and Law	Discrimination in hiring, firing, promotion, compensation, honors, rewards, and glass ceiling.
Countries	Ethnic cleansing, misusing aid, depriving people of basic needs, human rights, waging war, supporting terrorism.

Thoughts lead to words and then to action. If we can reduce the ripple of violence in our speech, that itself can make a huge impact on our audience. In our daily life, we inadvertently use many words and phrases which may invoke a negative thought or emotion. Our goal must be to use as much compassionate language as possible. We must think before we use words that evoke hatred, negativity, fear, and violence. As Mahatma Gandhi said, "You must be the change you want to see in the world." We must first start with our language and avoid words and phrases such as the following :

Violent phrases to avoid

- Many ways to skin a cat
- Kill two birds with one stone
- To kill time
- Shoot an email
- Shoot down an idea
- Kick around some ideas
- Throw the baby out with the bath water
- Drop a bombshell
- Crash and burn
- "Fire" somebody
- Silver bullet
- Head hunter
- It's to die for
- Killer application (instinct)
- Stupid

- Where is the beef?
- Don't put all your eggs in one basket
- Show me the beef
- Add some meat (to your presentation)
- Running around like a chicken with its head cut off
- This is just gravy
- Head count
- Dog eat dog
- Holy cow
- Black sheep of the family
- Take a shot at this
- Take a stab at this
- Sick
- Hate

"A human being is part of the whole that we call the universe, a part limited in time and space. He experiences himself, his thoughts and feelings, as something separated from the rest–a kind of optical illusion of his consciousness. This illusion is a prison for us, restricting us to our personal desires and to affection for only the few people nearest us. Our task must be to free ourselves from this prison by widening our circle of compassion to embrace all living beings and all of nature." — Albert Einstein

Source: Dr. Sulekh Jain

Food

Compassionate Healthy Diet

Jain Way of Life Food Pyramid

Throughout the day we eat a variety of food. Food governs not only our physical health but our mental well being and our social interactions. A Jain Way of Life diet minimizes harm to living beings. Jains believe that all living beings have Souls, unlike other traditions, who believe that only humans have Souls. Hence, killing of any living creatures, may it be a plant or a human being, is violence. However, Jains categorize living beings by the number of senses they possess (from one to five senses). The level of violence that is committed when any creature is harmed depends on the senses it possesses. For example, plants and bacteria are one-sense beings and cows, pigs or humans are five-sense beings. Eating meat is many orders of magnitude more violent than a plant based diet.

Diet Continuum

The practice of Non-Violence is on a continuum: likewise, vegetarianism is on a continuum or a scale, too. As you progress on your Jain Way of Life spiritual journey you become more vegetarian and then vegan. After limiting the types of food, Jains limit the variety and quantity of food and how food is prepared.

Meat, Fish	Jains completely refrain from this. Even "compassionate" individuals do not realize the violence that goes into the preparation of meat that is served on their plate. The brutality of slaughter houses has been distanced from the individuals who consume the meat. Silenced are the cries of billions of helpless animals led to death each day.
Eggs	Jains do not eat eggs because eggs hold the potential for life. When fertilized they produce five-sensed beings. Today, even unfertilized eggs are produced in inhumane conditions with chickens caged in coops the size of a shoe box and injected with antibiotics and hormones.
Milk and Dairy Products	Some Jains in North America avoid milk and dairy products and follow a vegan diet (vegetarian and no milk and dairy products). Cows are continuously pregnant and hormones are injected, and machines squeeze out the last drops of milk multiple times a day.

Root Vegetables	Some root vegetables like figs should be avoided as they have large numbers of insects in them.
Honey	Many bees are killed in the process of gathering it.
Liquor, Tobacco, and Drugs	Abstain from these intoxicants. These alter the state of mind which may lead one to cause violence via speech or action.
Fasting	Some level of fasting enhances spiritual well being. It purifies the body and the mind and brings freshness and agility. Fasting is done with pre-defined intentions – that of practicing an austerity to cleanse the body (not skipping meals due to convenience).
Daytime Eating	For thousands of years, Jains had taken vows to avoid night-time (after sunset) meals as part of their proactive use of Non-Violence. Small insects may be inadvertently killed during the preparation at night. Also, scriptures point out that growth of bacteria (one sense beings) is much higher at night. There are also medical benefits of daytime eating. Generally it is recommended not to sleep for 2 to 3 hours after a full meal in order to allow time for digestion.
Filtering Water	The scriptures define the exact method of filtering water using filter cloth and how it should be washed back into the source of water. This releases the trapped organisms back into their environment. Today much of the water supply is purified at the source as well as in our taps.

Jain Food Pyramid

Half a century ago when Jain and other vegetarian Indians came to North America, medical professionals considered them undernourished. Today Jain vegetarian diet is being emulated throughout the world. Below are the guidelines for a Jain Food Pyramid as modified based on data from the National Center for Nutrition and Dietetics, American Dietetics Associations, the 2005 USDA Dietary Guidelines for Americans, and USDA Food Guide Pyramid on www.mypyramid.gov.

Bread, Cereal, Rice and Pasta	6 ounces	Provides carbohydrates which are an efficient source of energy. Also, they provide fiber, protein, iron, and B vitamins.
Vegetable Group	2 1/2 cups	Starchy vegetables – such as potatoes, peas, etc. are higher in calories. Non-starchy, leafy green (spinach, cabbage, etc.) – high in calcium and are an essential part of a vegetarian diet. Deep green and deep yellow are high in carotenoids (vitamins for eyes). Non-starchy – Other Vegetables (tomatoes, cucumber, green beans, etc.)
Fruit Group	2 cups	Great source of vitamins A, C, and some B vitamins and minerals such as potassium. They are naturally low in fat. Some dried fruits are high in iron and vitamins.
Fats, Oils, and Sweets	6 teaspoons	This group of foods must be consumed sparingly. Indian traditional food contains very high unhealthy levels of this group.
Milk, Yogurt, Soy Milk	3 cups	Soy is a great substitute and source of protein, calcium, vitamin D, riboflavin, yet also tends to be high in cholesterol and saturated fats. A good substitution for this can be soymilk, soy yogurt and soy ice cream.
Dry Beans, Nuts, Legumes	5.5 ounces	There are three major forms of legumes: Dry beans include chickpeas, kidney beans, black eyed peas. Lentils include dried pigeon peas (toovar dal), masoor dal, and urad dal. Soy products include tofu, tempeh, soy yogurt, and soy milk. Nuts and seeds include almonds, peanut butter and sesame seed butter (tahini).

"Farmed animals are not future Buddhas donating their flesh out of compassion for those of us who have developed a craving for it. They are victims of our greed from whom we steal the most precious gift any of us has: life."
—Norm Phelps, The Great Compassion: Buddhism & Animal Rights

Source: Jain Food, "Compassionate and Healthy Eating," Manoj Jain MD, Laxmi Jain, Tarla Dalal

Responsible Food Purchasing

Food preparation begins with food purchasing. We must be mindful of how the food arrives in the grocery store, what the labeling on the package means, and what process the food has already been subjected to. In the Jain diet, food, from growth to consumption it, is treated in such a way as to minimize harm to living beings.

Growing fruits, vegetables, and grains requires energy (both manual and fossil fuel), water, land, artificial chemicals (pesticides, herbicides, and synthetic fertilizers), and labor. Canning, jarring, boxing, and bagging food into ready-to-eat products and transporting it requires more energy and natural resources. Most foods purchased in the United States travel 1,500-2,500 miles before reaching our plates; imported ingredients have longer journeys and more complex social and environmental histories. The choices you make at the grocery store affect people, animals, and places far away. Sustainable agriculture promotes good health, respect for animals and the environment, and social and economic well-being for communities and workers.

What Do All the Food Labels Mean?

Natural products are minimally processed and generally do not contain artificial ingredients, dyes, or preservatives.

Organic foods are grown without synthetic chemicals, pesticides, or fertilizers and exclude genetically modified ingredients. Organic dairy comes from cows that are raised without antibiotics and synthetic growth hormones, fed only organic feed, and have some access to the outdoors. Some studies estimate that organic farming uses 50% less energy than conventional methods.

Fair Trade certification guarantees farmers a minimum price for coffee, sugar, cocoa, etc. and additional premiums for organic products, enabling farmers to attain greater financial stability than by selling into the fluctuating commodities market. Fair Trade works directly with growers or through Fair Trade licensing organizations instead of through middlemen so farmers are paid a larger percentage of the retail price for their products.

Mindful Food Purchasing

Bring your own bags to the grocery store.
Buy fewer bagged vegetables (e.g., prewashed bagged lettuce).
Buy locally grown and seasonal produce and/or organic items. Try community supported agriculture (CSA), which consists of a group of people who support a farm as members or "shareholders" and, in return, receive weekly shares of fruits and vegetables from the farm.
Buy in bulk (to minimize packaging).
Shop at farmers' markets.
Choose Fair Trade products (sugar, cocoa, coffee, tea, and bananas are among the more available Fair Trade products).
Read the ingredients on packaged food, and opt for products with as few ingredients as possible. Try to avoid the following non-vegetarian animal ingredients: • Anything with EDTA (chemical preservative) • Mono – and diglycerides • Carmine (or cochineal) • Cysteine or l-cysteine • Gelatin • Bleached or bromated flour • High fructose corn syrup • Partially (and fully) hydrogenated fats • Methyl – or polyparaben • TBHQ (tertiary butylhydroquinone) • Animal rennet 
Buy unbleached flour; unrefined, unbleached (raw cane) sugar; and sea salt.
Buy fewer processed foods.
Avoid dairy if you can. If you must, choose certified organic dairy products, antibiotic/hormone-free milk, and/or milk from grass-fed cows. Do not consume eggs or egg-based products.

What to buy, Where to Buy it, and Other Resources

Grocery Stores: Whole Foods, Trader Joe's, and Wild Oats specialize in organic and sustainably produced foods. Most mainstream supermarkets also carry specialty natural and organic foods.

Farmers Markets: Find one near you: www.farmersmarkets.net

Locally Grown Produce: Find a Community Supported Agriculture (CSA) organization near you:
www.biodynamics.com/csa.html
www.localharvest.org/csa/
http://newfarm.org/farmlocator/index.php
www.wilson.edu/wilson/asp/content.asp?id=804

Fair Trade Products
www.transfairusa.org
www.equalexchange.com

Widely Available Brands for Everyday Food Products

Chocolate: Dagoba Organic, Divine Chocolate (www.divinechocolate.com), Endangered Species Organic, Green & Blacks, Newman's Own, Chocosphere (www.chocosphere.com)

Dairy: Oberweis Dairy (www.oberweisdairy.com), Organic Valley, Horizon Organic Valley, Stonyfield Farm, Silk.

Flour: King Arthur, Arrowhead Mills.

Cereal: Cascadian Farm, Back to Nature, Kashi, Nature's Path, Peace.

Margarine and oil: Soy Garden, Earth Balance, Spectrum Organics, anything cold-pressed or extra virgin.

Frozen and prepared foods: Cascadian Farm, Annie's Natural, Hain Celestial, Pacific, Garden of Eatin, Ethnic Gourmet, Eden, Bearitos, Newman's Own, Westbrae, Muir Glen, Yves.

Spices: Frontier, Simply Organic, and choose sea salt over conventional varieties.

"The beginning of mindful eating is the realization that eating meat is not about the meat-eater; it is about the animals who are tormented and killed." — The Great Compassion: Buddhism & Animal Rights, Norm Phelps

Writer: Megha Doshi

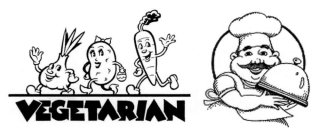

VEGETARIAN

Eating and Drinking Out and Enjoying: Best Practices

When it comes to eating cruelty-free in North America, today's options are endless. But confusion about food ingredients, not knowing where to find vegetarian-friendly restaurants, and uncertainty about meat-free meal preparation can hinder even the most committed vegetarian. For some, cooking a Jain meal can be spiritually uplifting and meditative, but eating out can be enjoyable and entertaining and a chance to try new tasty dishes.

Whatever the reason, if we follow Eating Out: Best Practices, we can enjoy clean, healthy vegetarian food without any mixing and contamination with non-vegetarian food. A simple rule of thumb is to eat out at vegetarian restaurants. Most major cities have at least serveal such restaurants where one of them is probably a South Indian, another will be Buddhist, and some will be American Vegan/Vegetarian/Heath Food.

Jain Eating Out Best Practices Guidelines

Roommate, spouse, friend, or relative	When staying or living with a companion, it will be easier to share a vegetarian meal if they are also vegetarian.
Conversation with a Waiter	Speak confidentially and politely, even if you are in a group of people. Let the waiter know, "I'm a strict vegetarian – I don't eat meat, fish, chicken, eggs, etc." "Can you recommend what you have on the menu that is strict vegetarian?" If the waiter still is unable to understand the request, let him know you are allergic to non-vegetarian food.
Soup	Ask the waiter, "Does the soup contain beef stock or lard?"
Frying Oil	"Do you know what type of oil this is fried in?" If the waiter hesitates (as many are new on the job), ask him, "Can you please double check with the chef?"
Pasta	Most pastas are egg based. Check with the waiter before you order.

Thai food	Confirm that the curries or other dishes do not have oyster or fish sauce. Also, specifically request that Pad Thai be made with no eggs.
Mexican	Some of the refried beans have lard. Also, some of the rice may have chicken broth.
Steak House	Even if you're stuck in a steak house, you have many options these days. You can ask them to make a vegetable stir fry or get multiple vegetable side dishes, salad, or potatoes.
Indian – Naan	Naans usually have eggs in them. If you're taking a buffet and Naan is the only option, ask for Roti. Be sure to leave a tip.
Chinese	Again, check for meat or fish sauce. Some of the rice may have a meat base.
Pizza	Some pizza sauce may be meat based and dough may have eggs. Ask them to use a washed clean knife to cut the pizza.
Tip	If the waiter provides excellent service, tip him or her 18% to 20%.
Deli/Sandwich shops (Subway, Quiznos, etc.)	These places provide some excellent options. Be careful that even veggie patties (at Subway, Burger King) are egg based. Ask them to prepare your sandwich on a clean surface/grill.
Fast Food Chains (McDonalds, Burger King, Wendy's, etc.)	Avoid these places whenever possible as you are endorsing food chains which are responsible for pushing meat consumption. Get a veggie burger, salad, apple pie, etc.
Donuts, Pastries, Cookies, etc.	Most of these contain eggs and you should avoid them. Some of the donuts are eggless.
Gloves and Knife	When possible let them know, "I'm a vegetarian – can you please change your gloves and clean the knife?"
Cheese w/rennet	Today rennet can be synthetic (chemical based) or can come from cows' guts. Avoid cheese with animal rennet.
Dressing	Mayonnaise, ranch, and most dressings have eggs. Try oil and vinegar dressing.
Ice Cream	Try to avoid ice cream if you don't know the ingredients as it may have eggs. Even fancy restaurants may offer soy.

Drinks

There are many wonderful non-alcoholic drinks to have when eating out.

Water	Simply water. Avoid carbonated water as it is not healthy.
Virgin (Non-Alcoholic) drinks	Most drinks such as Margaritas, Pina-Coladas can be made without alcohol.
Juices	Some juices (such as Tropicana Orange Juice, except for the ones marked with 'K') are fortified with Omega 3, which is derived from fish oil.
Lemonade	This is healthier than Coke or Pepsi.
Coke, Pepsi	Try to avoid these.
Beer	There is no shame or getting left out when you are not drinking a beer. There are many non-alcoholic drinks you can have.

Minimize Footprint

Vegetarian dishes may be seasoned with chicken stock, bacon bits, fish flavoring, oyster sauce or gelatin. Veggie burgers, delectable pizzas, grilled sandwiches or pasta heaped with veggies and extra sauce can be easily prepared at most restaurants. If requested with a big "vegetarian" smile on your face, you'll probably find that even the staunchest meat and potatoes chef will enjoy the challenge of preparing you a delicious and interesting vegetarian or vegan meal.

Although most Jain families eat out far less frequently than the average American, many Jains still enjoy going to restaurants once in a while and indulging in the occasional Taco Bell meal or latte from Starbucks. Considering the extent to which people dine out, it's important to minimize our social and environmental footprint when eating away from home.

What to buy, Where to buy it, and Other resources

Many restaurants serve sustainable foods. To find one near you, visit www.eatwellguide.org.

Sustainable offerings at well-known restaurants and cafes

Ben & Jerry's: Purchases milk from small family-owned farms that raise grass-fed cows without artificial hormones. Also uses Fair Trade certified cocoa and coffee; brownies from a nonprofit that focuses on social improvement; peanut butter from a company that offsets its CO2 emissions; and sustainably grown strawberries and vanilla. Serves dairy- and egg-free sorbets and some organic ice creams.

Caribou Coffee: Some Fair Trade and organic coffees (Rainforest Blend), supports coffee-growing communities by allocating funds to build clinics and schools, invests in reforestation and clean water programs, etc.

Chipotle: About 20% of beans served here are organic. Notable efforts to serve antibiotic-free, hormone-free, and organic ingredients.

Dunkin Donuts: Fair Trade coffee in all espresso beverages (not drip coffee)

Panera Bread: Organic cheese, yogurt, milk, and apple juice. Some organic ingredients in breads.

Peets Coffee: some organic coffees and teas, organic soy milk available, several social and environmental programs

Starbucks: Some organic and Fair Trade coffee, organic milk and soy milk available, organic Tazo teas, several social and environmental programs.

Simple Tips

- Hold the "extras" at fast food restaurants. Take only as many napkins, plastic silverware, single-serving condiments (e.g., Taco Bell salsa packets) as you need.

- Bring your own travel mug or reusable commuter cup to coffee shops. Your drink will stay hot (or cold) longer, and your responsible action will help keep millions of foam and paper cups out of landfills.

- Buy fewer bottled water and other bottled beverages.

- Avoid milk, cheese, butter, and eggs when possible. Don't be afraid to ask the waitstaff to alter menu items by removing dairy products. Many restaurants will happily accommodate vegetarians and vegans.

- Choose restaurants that use sustainably produced ingredients. In an ideal world, you should eat at restaurants that serve only vegetarian foods. If you do eat at a restaurant that also serves meat, try to patronize establishments that buy grass-fed, free-range, antibiotic- and hormone-free meat products. Spend your dining-out dollars at businesses that support sustainable agriculture.

- Choose family- and minority-owned or managed restaurants over chain establishments to promote economic development.

- Tip well for good service!

Bon Appetite!

"The Jain Sädhu leads a life which is praised by all. He practices the Vrats and rites strictly and shows to the world the way one has to go in order to realize the atma (Soul). Even the life of a Jain householder is so faultless that India should be proud of him."
— Dr. Satischandra Vidhya Bhushan

Writers: Rakesh Soni, Megha Doshi

Family

How to Raise a Jain Child

Parents' greatest wish is for their children to be happy, healthy, intelligent, successful, and selfless. It takes a core and extended family, community, culture, tradition, and religion and a responsible Way of Life to raise a child.

Practice of Jain Way of Life in thoughts, words, and actions insures happy, healthy, and balanced children. The following are some practical and effective actions which will help your children follow, internalize, and cherish a Jain Way of Life. This can be your gift to your children which will last a lifetime and will be carried through many generations.

Cake	Make it a point to purchase or make an eggless cake for your child when attending a birthday party (where cake with eggs will be served).
Temple	Must attend all temple functions. Make it interesting and rewarding for kids. Have your kids sit next to you during prayers and lectures and let them watch you and help you in volunteer work.
Lunch	Pack a tasty, healthy lunch or be sure that their school cafeteria serves it. Contact your local school food department and get their guidance.
Pathshala	Must attend pathshala or learn Jainism at home or online. Order Jain books.
Bug	When you or your child spots a bug or a mosquito in the home, gently remove it away and tell them that "*We don't kill living beings.*" Do not swat mosquitoes or use snap-traps for rodents.
Recycle	Do this with a passion and get the whole family involved.
Jai Jinendra	Greet family members in the morning with Jai Jinendra and even when greeting elders on the phone. Jai Jinendra means "I bow to the Soul in you and to Jinendra's Soul which has conquered itself of passions."
Homeless	Serve food, give clothes or volunteer for homeless people and get your child to actively participate.

Champagne and Drinking	Forget liquor, forget beer, forget wine, don't even take a sip of champagne at New Year's or any other function in front of your children or even otherwise. Be a model for them.
Big Deal – Celebrations	Make a big deal of functions and festivals at home. Celebrate with passion. Get children involved. Invite friends, family and local college students.
Deep Respect	Give deep respect, care, and attention to elders. Touch their feet. Greet them with Jai Jinendra when talking on the telephone.
Mother and Father respect each other	Let your children see and hear you respecting your spouse and your parents. By seeing this example, the child will learn to respect others.
Trip	Visit Jain temples and other spiritual places when visiting another city. Go to India often and visit Jain Pilgrimage.
Monks and Nuns	Invite monks, nuns, and scholars home. Get children to help in serving them.
Prayers	Even if for 3 minutes, do prayer and quiet meditation every evening. Do it together with the family. Make this part of your daily routine. Visit local temples. Give money to kids to donate each time.
Language	Teach one or more languages of the parents/grandparents.
Paryushan	Make a huge deal of Paryushan-Das Lakshan and follow it with zeal (See Paryushan point sheet section).
Resolution	Make a yearly resolution. Get ideas from this book.
Dating	Kids will ask many questions regarding dating, going out late, etc. You should let them know that until appropriate marriageable age, we don't need to date. Have alternative activities for them.
Friends	Open your home to your children's friends — this will give you a chance to know them. Have plenty of food and healthy snacks.
Rides	Whenever possible, instead of other people picking up your teenagers, volunteer to pick up your kids (and other kids) from school activities, movies, eating out, etc. Be ready 24x7 to give your kids a ride.
Relatives	Meet often with relatives. Take the time to understand their positive actions and behavior. Let them be role models. Be sure that the kids pay respect to them as well.
Arguments	Never argue or fight in front of kids. They feel tremendous mental violence by observing their parents angry at each other.
Banned words	Ban these words at home: Hate, Shut up, Stupid, Crazy, Dumbo etc.

Money and Kids

By Sudha Murthy, author and wife of Infosys Chairman Narayan Murthy.

The greatest difficulty in having money is to teach your children its value. Bringing up children in a moneyed atmosphere is a difficult task. Even today, I think twice if I have to spend Rs.10 on an auto when I can walk to my house. I cannot expect my children to do the same. They have seen money from the time they were born. But we can lead by example. When they see Murthy wash his own plate after eating and clean the two toilets in the house every day, they realize that no work is demeaning, irrespective of how rich you are. This doesn't mean we expect our children to live an austere life. My children buy what they want, go where they want, but they have to follow certain rules. They have to show me bills for whatever they buy: My daughter can buy five new outfits, but she has to give away five old ones. My son can go out with his friends for lunch or dinner, but we discourage him from going to a five star hotel.

Punish the Child or Punish Yourself

By: Dr. Arun Gandhi, grandson of Mahatma Gandhi

I was 16 years old and living with my parents at the institute my grandfather had founded 18 miles outside of Durban, South Africa, in the middle of the sugar plantations. We were deep in the country and had no neighbors, so my two sisters and I would always look forward to going to town to visit friends or go to the movies.

One day, my father asked me to drive him to town for an all-day conference; I jumped at the chance. Since I was going to town, my mother gave me a list of groceries she needed and as I had all day in town my father asked me to take care of several pending chores, such as getting the car serviced. When I dropped my father off that morning, he said, "I will meet you here at 5:00 p.m., and we will go home together."

After hurriedly completing my chores, I went straight to the nearest movie theatre. I got so engrossed in a John Wayne double-feature that I forgot the time. It was 5:30 before I remembered. By the time I ran to the garage and got the car and hurried to where my father was waiting for me, it was almost 6:00. He anxiously asked me, "Why were you late?"

I was so ashamed of telling him I was watching a John Wayne western movie that I said, "The car wasn't ready, so I had to wait," not realizing that he had already called the garage.

When he caught me in the lie, he said, "There's something wrong in the way I brought you up that didn't give you the confidence to tell me the truth. In order to figure out where I went wrong with you, I'm going to walk home 18 miles and think about it." So, dressed in his suit and dress shoes, he began to walk home in the dark on mostly unpaved, unlit roads.

I couldn't leave him, so for five-and-a-half hours I drove behind him, watching my father go through this agony for a stupid lie that I uttered. I decided then and there that I was never going to lie again. I often think about that episode and wonder, if he had punished me the way we punish our children, whether I would have learned a lesson at all. I don't think so. I would have suffered the punishment and gone on doing the same thing.

But this single Non-Violent action was so powerful that it is still as if it happened yesterday. That is the power of Non-Violence.

> *"Samyag-darshana-jnana-charitrani mokshmargah – Goal of human life is liberation and the path to liberation is through Enlightened Intuition, Enlightened Knowledge and Enlightened Conduct"* — Tattvarth Sutra by Umäsväti

Writers: Preeti Jain, Yogendra Jain

Marriage Commitment – A Conversation

Marriage can dramatically change your life direction, beliefs, practices and way of life, and affects many generations to come. Your Jain Way of Life (JWOL) practice can be strengthened or be severely setback depending on whom you marry. Hence, it is important that you have a conversation on critical issues when contemplating a serious relationship leading to marriage. Unique life experiences and upbringing, coupled with religious practices, determine ones outlook. No two people will align on all issues but there are some critical issues that you may not wish to compromise on. Also, a relationship has an intangible element called "chemistry." Sometimes chemistry in a potential relationship overpowers parents' reasoning and guidance. Even when the chemistry appears to match and all stars appear to align, it is always a good idea to have a *conversation*.

The following are guidelines for a heart to heart *conversation* with a potential life partner to affirm living a JWOL (Jain Way of Life) for the rest of your lives.

"Conversation" on Critical Issues

Issue	Jain Way of Life Practice	A conversation with a Jain or a non-Jain potential spouse
Diet	Strict vegetarian	Common dietary habits are so integral to any relationship. Can we agree that there will be no non-vegetarian food ever brought in the home or consumed outside? This is critical to me. Also, my vegetarian family and relatives visiting will be much more comfortable.
Kids	Raised as strict vegetarian	Kids will be raised as strict vegetarians. This is a healthy and compassionate diet.
Alcohol	No consumption	No alcohol will be brought and kept in the home, and we both will not consume any alcohol outside of the home as well.

Issue	Jain Way of Life Practice	A conversation with a Jain or a non-Jain potential spouse
Religion	Jainism and Jain Way of Life	We both may come from different traditions – we may follow our respective religions and will share them with each other and with our kids.
Kids Religious Upbringing	Jain Way of Life	Our kids will follow a Jain Way of Life, as this is very much in alignment with other beliefs and traditions. Of course, we can follow other traditions as well as long as they do not compromise our vegetarian and Non-Violent practice. Also, the kids will attend a Jain Pathshala (Jain education classes).
Hunting, Fishing	No violence	We agree that we will not hunt and fish.
Bugs	Gently take them outside	If we find bugs in the home, we will gently shoo the bugs away and not swat them.
Gambling	No	We will avoid gambling. Even if we go to casinos, etc. we will keep a reasonable limit of say $100 or so and play within that limit.
Fur, Leather	No	We will not buy a car with leather seats, jackets, or furniture; nor will we use leather belts, shoes, or handbags.
Donation	2-3% of our annual income	We will donate to organizations that actively promote Non-Violence.

"Conversation" on Less Critical Issues

Issue	Jain Way of Life View	A conversation with a Jain or a non-Jain potential spouse
Eggs, etc.	No eggs, gelatin, dairy products, etc. (in today's world, eggs and dairy products cause similar levels of violence)	I will not consume eggs, gelatin, honey, etc.
Pets	Avoid having pets as we do not want to keep them in bondage.	If we do decide to get pets, we will feed them a vegetarian diet. We will not neglect them and treat them as members of the family.
Language	Learn at least one native language	We will teach at least one native language to our kids.
Job	Aligned with JWOL	We will avoid jobs that cause violence to humans and animals.
Volunteer	Provide social service	We will offer our volunteer service based on our time and ability.
Environment	Recycle, use a hybrid car	We will try our best to recycle as much as possible, purchase cars and other necessary things which are environmentally friendly.
Animal Tested Products	Minimize use of animal-tested products; seek alternatives	We will avoid animal tested products as much as possible.
Prayers before a Meal	Increase spirituality	We will do a short Jain prayer and another prayer (that a spouse of different faith may prefer) before a meal.

"I believe that we are all endowed with a spirit or a Soul. Together with you, I would like to live a life of Non-Violence, Non-Absolutism, and Non-Possessiveness ... so we can be happy, our kids can be happy, and we can share this happiness with the world." —[Your Name Here]

A Typical Day – Jain Way of Life

We pass through many stages in life and our typical daily activities and priorities change. However, the core of our typical day can be grounded in a Way of Life which is mindful, compassionate, and able to increase our spiritual strength.

Be sure that once every hour you take a long deep breath lasting at least 15 seconds.

The following are typical day activity highlights:

Activity	Recommendation
Wake Up	Wake up early. With your palms together and sitting with your back straight, take three deep breaths.
Prayer	Say Namokar Mantra three times.
Brush/Shave	Do not leave the water running. Turn the lights off. Save energy.
Shower	Seven minute shower (with non-animal tested soap, shampoo, conditioner, etc.).
Prayers	After shower say Namokar Mantra once; one prayer/stuti, and do three minutes of meditation.
Breakfast	Soymilk, fruits, cereal, whole wheat bread toast/bagel.
Heat/Lights	Before leaving home for school or work, be sure to turn the heat down and lights out as these energy sources are environmentally unfriendly. Keep home heat (even if it is free and included in the rent) down to 65 degrees average temperature in the winter and 80 degrees in the summer.
Driving	Take three deep breaths when pulling out of your driveway (or home). Drive with mindfulness, relax in traffic, and avoid road rage. Look forward to a red light—it will give you an opportunity to relax.
'RoadKill'	When you see a dead animal on the road, take a moment to say Namokar Mantra and ask for forgiveness.
Lunch	Say Namokar Mantra once before you eat.

Each Hour	Relax, stretch the body once every hour and do deep breathing (15 seconds long) several times each hour.
Work/Study	Respect others' views; keep Non-Absolutism in mind; control anger and criticism; be humble, friendly and compassionate.
Exam/Meeting	Before starting, take three deep breaths, stretch, and relax your body. Do not cheat.
On Dinner Table	Start with Namokar Mantra and say it mindfully.
Dinner	Eat a healthy, tofu, protein-based balanced meal. Eat until you reach only 75% of a full stomach. Eat fresh vegetables/meals when possible. Avoid garlic, onions, and if possible, potatoes.
Dishes/Cleaning	All family members help in cleanup. Minimize water wastage. Use non-animal tested detergent.
Recycling	Recycle every little item (newspaper, boxes, plastic bottles, cans, office papers, etc.).
Evening Classes	Learn a new activity or take an evening course.
Evening	Do 10-minute prayers with family (2 minute relaxation, 3 minute prayers, 5 minute guided meditation).
Before Sleeping	Read a spiritual book for a minimum of 5 minutes every day before you go to sleep.
Bed Time	Go to bed early so you can rise early.
Laundry	Minimize loads/washes; conserve water; dry large towels, bedsheets, etc. in the sun if possible; Use biodegradable, non-animal tested detergent.
Sunday	Attend Pathshala; go to temple; do prayers at home or in a group.
Media	Watch educational shows, light comedy, and news on TV/Internet. Avoid violent and scandalous shows.
Soap Opera	Since these are emotionally charged and passionate, avoid them.
Internet	Monitor frequently as the kids surf the Internet
Video Games	Do not purchase any violent video games or let kids play with these. Tell them why so that they will not play these games at other children's houses.
Pollution in your town	Be aware of the air you breathe and toxins in your community. See what precautions you can take by visiting http://www.scorecard.org.

"Battle with yourself! Of what use is fighting others? He who conquers himself gets eternal bliss" — Uttaradhyayan Sutra

Contributor: Priyanka Jain

Vacations, Retreats, and Camps

Going on vacations and retreats is important for relaxation, learning about the world, and being together with family and friends. In addition to tingling our senses and emotions, some parts of the vacation should include appeal to the mind and the Soul. This can be quite an exhilarating experience. Vacations should also be a time to reflect about ourselves, our practices, and our habits. In the United States as well as all over the world, there are thousands of vacation spots and retreats which are not only fun but also spiritually uplifting.

Retreats One type of vacation is a retreat, where you leave the tensions and responsibilities of your daily life, and go to a place closely associated with nature and learning. More specifically, there are places which are religious retreats. Here you can immerse in beautiful temples, nature, rituals, scriptural learning, meditation, yoga, herbal treatment, and more. In the United States, Jain retreats include the serene Siddachalam (in New Jersey), where they have cabins and ample accommodations and delicious vegetarian meals.

Jain temples in United States and retreats in India Almost every major U.S. city and most Indian cities have one or many Jain temples (See list of Jain Temples on page 178). You can visit many of the other great temples in the country, such as, Jain Center of Southern California and Northern California, Detroit, New York, Boston, Toronto, Chicago, Houston, and many more cities. Even vacation hot spots such as Las Vegas and Florida have Jain temples. There are thousands of Jain pilgrimages and retreats in India with breathtaking scenery, and grand ancient temples.

Jain Camps Siddhachalam and various Jain Centers keep a Jain Camp yearly. Here you can enjoy activities such as yoga, meditation, hiking, sports and hearing interesting lectures. While going trekking, you can jointly sing Namokar Mantra and stutis together for the first 10 minutes of the hike, or practice total meditative silence. To minimize trampling on small plants and killing small insects, you want to take extra precautions while exploring nature.

Create your Own Several families can get together and plan their own customized spiritual retreat. Each member can be asked to prepare a talk on a subject or a book they have read and others can help in meditation and prayers, etc.

Visiting Friends and Family Visiting family and friends in the United States or India is always a nice change and can be immensely enjoyable. Take these visits as a chance to understand "good practices" that they have incorporated into their lives. Be sure to help your host with all household activities (cooking, cleaning, making beds, helping with children) so that their work by having you there is reduced.

The following are recommendations:

Camping	Excellent way to experience nature. Avoid campfires as firewood has many insects living in them. If you must, then tap the wood vertically to dislodge insects and worms. Avoid eating out at night.
U.S. Cities	Visit a Jain temple and also visit famous temples and churches.
Other Countries	Visit famous churches, sight–seeing landmarks, cultural events, holy sites, etc.
Hiking	Practice silence for a few minutes; walk carefully to minimize killing of insects.
Museum	Understand the many views (multiplicity of views). Visit the Holocaust, Natural History, Art, Science museums and understand the diverse viewpoints.
In the Car	Play some religious and devotional music for some time. Meditate together. The best time is when you start your journey in the morning.
Yoga/Meditation Retreats	Art of Living offers courses in practical wisdom on how to live gracefully in a stressful world, and also the deep spiritual experience necessary to put that knowledge into action.
Casinos	Enjoy the casinos, see the architecture, see the people obsessed with gambling, smoking and drinking. See the human behavior. If you must gamble, set a limit of $20 to $50 per day and vow to gamble no more than that.
Recycling	Use paper plates whenever possible. Put your name on cups so they can be reused.

"Every variety of living creature I must ever defend from harm." — Ta-chwang-yan-ling-lun (sermon 62)

Contributor: Sonia Shah

Very Responsible Purchasing

Jain core practice of Non-Violence extends far beyond being vegetarian and avoiding activities that hurt insects. The products we buy, how we use them, and how we dispose of them are important opportunities for Jains to practice Non-Violence and Non-Possessiveness. Most Jains are familiar with what happens on farms and in slaughter houses to make meat and leather products. Similarly, it is important to understand how other everyday products – such as food, electronics, jewelry, and clothing – are manufactured. Some of these processes inflict violence on people, animals, and the environment in the form of poor labor conditions, human rights abuses, pollution, inefficient use of resources, health risks, and social and economic injustice. We all must eat, wear clothes, and use technology every day to function as productive citizens and Jains. Since lay Jains are neither able to nor expected to eliminate all violence from our lives, we should instead focus on becoming more aware of the social and environmental consequences of our purchases and seek to minimize the overall impact of our lives. The following pages provide a primer on the main issues associated with everyday products. A wealth of information is readily available online. It's up to you to become aware of the impacts of the products you use and seek out ways to integrate Non-Violence and Non-Possessiveness into your shopping and consumption decisions.

About Jewelry

Families regularly purchase jewelry without realizing the social and environmental implications of gold and diamond mining and production. While the jewelry industry helps generate revenues for developing countries, gold and diamond production pollutes the air, water, and land; contributes to military conflict; leads to human rights atrocities; and generates tons of toxic waste. Keep in mind the following information when purchasing gold and diamond jewelry:

- Producing one gold ring requires 30 tons of ore and generates 20 tons of mine waste.

- More than 50% of the world's diamonds are processed in India, where many of the cutters and polishers are bonded child laborers who work to pay off the debts of their relatives, often unsuccessfully.

- Roughly 4%-10% of the world's diamonds are known as "conflict diamonds." These diamonds are traded by rebel soldiers and governments to finance military activities, buy weapons, and fuel civil strife. The majority of conflict diamonds come from Angola, Liberia, Sierra Leone, and Congo.

Simple Tips

- Minimize your jewelry purchases.

- When you do purchase gold and diamonds, make sure that the jewelry you're buying was produced responsibly. Use the Internet and the resources in the next column to make informed decisions.

- If your family has old jewelry sets that are no longer worn, try recycling them into new pieces. Many jewelers, especially Indian jewelers, will melt down your old gold jewelry and reuse the diamonds to make brand new custom pieces. This is a cheaper and more sustainable alternative to purchasing new jewelry.

- Many jewelers carry vintage jewelry, including engagement/wedding rings.

- Up to 15% of the world's rough diamonds come from small-scale informal digging activities which are often unlicensed and exploited by rebel military groups.

Useful Resources

Brilliant Earth (www.brilliantearth.com): All diamonds are harvested and finished using fair trade practices and are certified conflict-free by third-parties. 5% of profits goes to the Diamonds for Africa Fund.

Adia Diamonds (www.adiadiamonds.com): Makes high-quality diamonds in a laboratory. All diamonds are conflict-free and produced in an environmentally friendly way.

Tiffany & Co. (www.tiffany.com): Played a major role in establishing a system adhered to by trading countries and the jewelry industry to keep conflict diamonds out of the legitimate diamond supply. Tiffany is among 11 jewelry retail companies that support the No Dirty Gold campaign's "Golden Rules," which were introduced in 2006 and establish principles for socially and environmentally responsible gold mining.

About Clothing

Public awareness has increased about sweatshops and poor labor conditions at textile and apparel factories. Many large brand name companies outsource their clothes manufacturing to sweatshops that have poor wages and benefits and appalling working conditions. Through our clothing purchases, we can encourage clothing retailers and manufacturers to improve labor rights at their suppliers' factories and promote economic empowerment and community development.

Useful Resources

Co-op America's Clothing Retailer Scorecard
www.coopamerica.org/programs/sweatshops/scorecard.cfm
Responsible Shopper
www.coopamerica.org/programs/rs/companies.cfm
Non-leather shoes, belts, and accessories
www.veganshoes.com
www.mooshoes.com
www.alternativeoutfitters.com
www.veganessentials.com
www.earthshoes.com
www.thevegetariansite.com
www.newbalance.com
www.ethicalwares.com
www.vegetarianshoesandbags.com
www.planetshoes.com
American Apparel (www.americanapparel.net): Manufactures all garments in company-owned factories in Los Angeles. Offers competitive wages, generous employee benefits, and stable employment to its textile factory workers. Also sells clothing made from organic cotton.
Gaiam (www.gaiam.com): Clothing made from organic cotton and other natural products.

Nike (www.nike.com): Nike Organics line includes 95-100% organic cotton clothing. About half of Nike's cotton products are made from 5% organic cotton, and the company has eliminated virtually all toxic chemicals in the rubber components of its footwear.

No Sweat Apparel (www.nosweatapparel.com): Sells 100% union-made apparel and footwear. Union workers generally have more job security and better wages and benefits than non-union workers.

Patagonia (www.patagonia.com): Donates 1% of profits to environmental causes. By using recycled bottles in some clothing, Patagonia has saved 86 million bottles from landfills.

Timberland (www.timberland.com): Timberland shirts sold in the United States contain at least 6% cotton. The company's goal was for organic cotton to account for 5% of its total cotton purchasing in 2005. It has developed footwear using less water and energy, environmentally preferred materials such as recycled

Simple Tips

- Minimize your clothing purchases. This includes American clothes as well as Indian clothes. Think hard before you purchase another sari, Panjabi, etc.

- Buy clothes at thrift shops and exchange clothes with friends and relatives.

- Buy high-quality clothing that will last longer.

- Use online resources (see adjacent column) to find socially responsible clothing companies.

- Avoid leather, silk, and fur.

- Buy organic cotton clothing and textiles when you can. Conventionally grown cotton is among the world's most pesticide-intensive crops. Buying a 100% organic cotton T-shirt over a non-organic one saves 1/3 lb. of synthetic fertilizers and pesticides from entering the waste stream.

rubber, and no polyvinyl chloride. The company has proactively addressed labor issues and employee welfare at its overseas and suppliers' facilities.

Gap (www.gap.com): Is a leader in the apparel industry for addressing labor rights violations in its supply chain. Several labor rights groups have praised Gap's factory monitoring and compliance systems. All proceeds from GAP Project Red Jeans go to the Global Fund for Africa.

About Electronics

Appliances and electronics have become so inexpensive that people are buying new gadgets and PCs left and right without adequately understanding the impact of their purchases. Keep in mind the following:

1) **How the products are manufactured.**

   Electronic products contain hundreds of materials, many of which are toxic-heavy metals and pollutants such as lead, mercury, cadmium, beryllium, hazardous chemicals, and polyvinyl chloride (PVC). These substances pollute the land, air, and water when electronics are not discarded properly. Workers, especially children and pregnant women, face health risks when exposed to lead and mercury when manufacturing these products in factories.

2) **How the products are used.**

   Electronics naturally require energy to operate. Most energy in the United States and is derived from burning coal and oil, which generates greenhouse gas emissions and contributes to climate change. Between 60% and 80% of the electricity used by most appliances is sucked away when they're not even being used. Light displays (like the lights on your computer monitors and printers) and "instant on" features (like the ability of the remote control to "talk" to the TV) use energy all day long.

3) How the products are discarded?

Increased purchasing of electronic goods results in more products being thrown away – a problem known as e-waste. Mobile phones have a lifecycle of less than two years. The average lifespan of computers in developed countries dropped from six years in 1997 to just two years in 2005. In 2004, less than 1 in 30 home computers was recycled. When thrown away, these electronics end up in landfills or incinerators. Since electronics contain heavy metals and hazardous chemicals, discarding or burning them releases lead, cadmium, and mercury into the air and ashes. Mercury released into the atmosphere can bioaccumulate in the food chain, If the products contain PVC plastic, highly toxic dioxins and furans are also released.

Useful Resources

GreenMachine Desktops (www.greenmachineshop.com). One-stop shopping for eco friendly computers and accessories. Also offers a free e-class on buying efficient PCs.

ENERGY STAR (www.energystar.gov/index.cfm?fuseaction=find_a_product): Comprehensive resource for information on energy-efficient electronics and appliances. Energy Star is a U.S. government program that provides guidelines and promotes best practices for energy-efficient homes and businesses.

EPEAT (www.epeat.net): Excellent resource for energy-efficiency and environmental ratings for desktops, laptops, and monitors. Maintained by the Green Electronics Council.

HP: Through its Planet Partners program, HP offers pickup, transportation, evaluation for reuse or donation, and recycling for a wide variety of its products, ranging from PCs to printer, scanners, and print cartridges.

Dell: Will pick up your old computer, regardless of the brand, for recycling or donation. Dell also uses up to 25% post-industrial recycled plastics in its desktop computer, portable computer, and server chassis plastics.

Toshiba: Will trade in your old (functioning) Toshiba equipment and will give you a discount on a new Toshiba. The company recycles and reuses old parts. http://toshiba.eztradein.com/toshiba/

Phillips: Launched its EcoDesign program in 1994 to minimize product weight, reduce packaging, increase recyclables and lifespan, and optimize energy efficiency.

Panasonic: (made by Matsushita): Manufactures more than 475 ENERGY STAR products under its Panasonic brand name. Homes equipped with Panasonic energy-efficient appliances could emit 34% fewer greenhouse gas emissions from 1991 levels, a remarkable achievement considering that the average household used 14 times more appliances in 2005 than 1991.

General resources on socially responsible companies and products:

New Dream's Conscious Consumer Marketplace:
www.newdream.org/consumer/marketplace.php

Better World Travel:
http://betterwoldtravel.com

Responsible Shopper:
www.coopamerica.org/programs/rs/

Treehugger:
www.treehugger.com

Simple Tips

- Minimize your electronics purchases. Just because your cell phone company offers a free new phone after one year, or a new printer or TV is on sale, don't feel you need to accumulate more electronics.

- Use a toaster oven or crockpot over electric stove tops or gas and electric ovens. Toaster ovens use up to 50% less energy than full-sized electric ovens. Microwaves are more efficient than gas and electric ovens but less efficient than gas stove tops.

- When choosing a computer, buy a laptop over a desktop. Although generally more expensive than desktops, laptops use 75 – 100 fewer watts than desktops.

- Chose a low-energy computer to save up to $300 per year in energy costs and use up to 70% less energy than standard computers.

- Choose a flat-panel monitor for TVs and computers – they use up to 30% less energy and contain far less lead than the older cathode ray tube (CRT) monitors.

- Save energy and money by setting your computer to "sleep mode" and turning it off overnight – this saves an additional $25-$75/yr. (New PCs are designed to handle more than 100 years' worth of on/off cycles.)

- Recycle your old PCs and other electronic equipment.

- Unplug appliances (like TVs, computers, etc.) when you're not using them. In the average home, 40% of all electricity is used to power home appliances while they're turned off.

- Recycle regular alkalines and rechargeable batteries.

- Buy compact fluorescent light bulbs (CFL) instead of standard incandescent bulbs. By replacing a 100-watt bulb with its CFL equivalent, you'll save $100+ in electricity costs over the lifetime of each bulb because CFLs use 90-95% less energy and last up to 15 times longer. If you replace ten 100W light bulbs with CFLs, you'll reduce the same amount of CO_2 that an SUV emits over a year.

"Jainism presents various solutions of the ecological problem through its focus on Non-Violence. Jains hold that not only humans and animals but also earth, air, fire, and vegetables are also sentient and living beings (or harbor them). For Jains to pollute, to disturb, to hurt, and to destroy them means committing violence against them." — Professor Sagarmal Jain

Contributor: Megha Doshi
See *Business Week's* expose: "Secrets, Lies, and Sweatshops," www.businessweek.com/magazine/content/06_48/b4011001.htm, Nov. 27, 2006 for more information.

Guidelines to Donations and Gift Giving

Jains have a rich tradition of philanthropy. However, as the pressures of daily living, paying for children's education, and health increase, we forget the critical role that Jain Way of Life organizations play in strengthening our family and religious values. These organizations are competing against mass media and don't have the financial prowess to compete for your money. It is for this reason that we must take every opportunity to proactively donate money to these organizations. Even today in some traditions, up to 10% of income is donated to a church, temple, or religious charities. The following are some guidelines:

Annual Donation – Budget 2% to 5% of family income:

A family should budget 2%-5% of their income for donation. The actual amount that goes out of pocket is in fact 30% – 40% less than this amount as you can take deduction in your taxes.

For Parents with Working Children: Your working children probably have strong stable jobs but do not have the time to donate. You can be proactive and have them donate jointly with you or inform them of organizations they can donate to. This will continue the tradition of donations in future generations.

Example: For a family with $100K per year joint income, donation at 5% salary level is $5,000 and 2% level is $2,000 which can be balanced as follows:

In order to qualify for a tax deduction, be sure that the organization is registered under IRS Section 501 (C) (3) as a Non-Profit Tax Exempt Organization.

Recommendations for a Family with $100K / Year Income

Donation to	% Allocation	5% Donation Double-income or single family	2% Donation Family with kids in college
Local Jain Centers/Temples /Sanghs	30%	$1,500	$600
JAINA Organization	30%	$1,500	$600
Animal Rights /Protection Group	10%	$500	$200
Charity/Education in India	15%	$750	$300
Local U.S. Charity	15%	$750	$300

Planned Giving

Through strong education and work ethic, many of you are affluent. Some of you have spent your lifetime acquiring wealth through hard work and long hours. However, most of you have not taken the time to formulate a well-designed plan to distribute your wealth. When arranging a team of individuals to help many of you plan estates, the three most frequently discussed issues are how to:

1. Secure the livelihood of a spouse

2. Maximize the distribution to heirs

3. Minimize the estate tax.

When these issues arise, you are pitting two objectives against one another: How can wealth be preserved in the family? How can taxes be reduced simultaneously? Without proper planning, the more wealth you leave for your family, the more estate taxes need to be paid. Philanthropy, however, can be used to reduce taxes and simultaneously help involve family members and transmit values.

Philanthropy gives value to wealth. If the wealth holder computes what is needed for support, for education of children, for amenities and for contingencies of market action or personal circumstances, he or she may well conclude there is more wealth than is "needed" and might reasonably look beyond consumption. With philanthropy, wealth can be valuable even when not used for personal consumption. Wealth can be used to benefit others, bring one more meaning to one's life, and to connect with a community. Parents engaging in charitable giving, whether through gifts or volunteerism, can model for children how wealth can be used wisely and selflessly.

Charitable Giving-Benefits to the Donor

1. Serve the community.

2. Share values with the family, children and grandchildren and leave a legacy.

3. Retain income for your lifetime or provide an income for loved ones.

4. Pass on a significant portion of your assets to children/ grandchildren.

5. Income tax reduction.

6. Gift tax, estate tax, capital gains tax, generation skipping tax reduction/elimination.

The U.S. tax laws generally are very favorable to generous people. They allow donors to receive many tax deductions that at the same time benefit their next generation as well as charitable organizations.

What Can You Give?

A donor can give **1.** Cash and cash equivalents, **2.** Publicly traded securities, **3.** Closely held securities, **4.** Life insurance, **5.** Real estate, **6.** Personal property, **7.** Retirement assets, **8.** In-kind gifts and pro bono services.

How Can You Give?

	Recipient Organization Benefit	Donor Benefit
Cash and cash Equivalents	Receive donations	May take a charitable gift deduction for the amount of a charitable gift of cash or cash equivalents.
Life Insurance	Receive significantly large charitable gifts	Can deduct the premium as donors pay them. Also can deduct the cash value.

	Recipient Organization Benefit	Donor Benefit
An outright gift of appreciated marketable securities	Receives donations	A charitable value of the security on the date of the gift, provided the donor owned it for more than one year. In addition, a donor does not incur capital gains tax on the transfer of such securities.
A Charitable Lead Trust	Receives an income stream for a specified length of time.	The capital value of marketable or income producing assets to remain in the donor's family. This is a unique and efficient way of passing the donor's assets to the next generation.
A Charitable Remainder Trust	Receives the principal at the end	A donor retains defined income interest for their lifetime and a large income tax deduction now. The trust can sell appreciated security and at the same time no capital gains tax on the realized gain.
A Bequest	Generally bequests have been the main source of endowment support.	A bequest would qualify a donor's estate for an estate tax charitable deduction equal to the entire amount one bequeath.

Jains are the largest donor group in India. We have a unique opportunity to live a Jain Way of Life and share this with our fellow North Americans. A donation to Jain organizations such as JAINA (which is registered under IRS Section 501 (C) (3) as a Non-Profit Tax Exempt Religious Organization) allows the organization to:

1. Provide funding to promote Non-Violence and peace all over the world
2. Assist and promote charitable and humanitarian community services in North America and worldwide
3. Create funding and resources to establish an endowed chair in Jain studies at various American colleges and universities
4. Support projects which share the Jain Way of Life.

A Note or a Plaque when Donating to Non-Jain Organizations

When you or your organization is donating and you have an option to place a message or a plaque, perhaps you can frame a message as follows :

Donated by JAIN Center (or Shah Family)

JAINISM is a Religion and a Way of Life.

JAINS practice Non-Violence, compassion, respecting other views, vegetarianism, balancing possessions, and self-realization.

"Take control of your desires and passions and you will enrich the quality of your happiness; submit to desires, and you will invite pain." — Mulachar

Contributor: Jaina Planned Giving Committee – Yogesh Kamdar – Chairman

Self and Work

Excelling in the Workplace

Great Corporate Leaders Practice Jain Core Values

Are you happy and engaged at your job? Are you using your best strengths and developing them into your recognized core competencies? Does your boss praise you and recognize your work? Or are you frustrated with the quarreling, turf wars, and endless delays in decision making in your workplace?

Internalizing and practicing our core Jain values helps us excel in our work place and greatly enhances the environment for team work and higher productivity. Evaluate your corporate leaders – are they are following these Jain core values?

The table below shows how you can apply core Jain values to excel in many workplace situations.

(Core Values of NV=Non-Violence; NA=Non-Absolutism; NP=Non-Possessiveness)

Tools/ Situations	My Actions	Core Values
Meetings	Do not cling to your opinions and ideas, be flexible enough to change your stance. Listen to everyone and accept that the solution can be obtained by many paths.	NP – Let go of attachment to one's thoughts or standpoint, which really are the hardest to give up since they stem from one's ego (also NA).
Ideas	Understand that each person has a unique perspective. Let people openly discuss, and share, ideas which often lead to a far superior solution.	NA – Recognize that everything is not black and white and there is room for difference in opinions.
Team Work	To avoid conflicts, have an open minded view of things and a feeling of acceptance/respect that other team members' views could also be correct. Strive for win-win. Be mindful of your ego.	NA – Thinking in absolute terms will lead to disengaging of others on the team.

Tools/ Situations	My Actions	Core Values
Email	Never use written words to defame/blame others as they have a tendency to multiply and spread.	NV – Not hurting by thought, word or deed.
Personal	When at work, focus on work. Avoid stealing work time for personal activities. Minimize bringing your personal worries/problems into your work time.	NP – Be less possessive of your worries/personal activities and let them go during work time.
Overworking	In the process of giving too much importance to your work, do not forget the other aspects of life. Try to move beyond one's ego-bound self to a greater realization of the larger, all-encompassing Self.	NP – We must balance our possessions and time, and prioritize how our time and energy spent.
Managing	Take the time to listen – genuinely listen – to others to understand their views.	NA – Respect that every person is entitled to his own opinion, which may be the right one.
Decisions	Integrate perspective and formulate a new and better solution. Credit others.	NP
Salary	Understand from many viewpoints your salary and have realistic expectations. Do not jump from one company to another for small salary increase.	NP – Learn to live with fewer possessions. NA – See company's view and your capabilities and experiences, and manage your salary expectations.
Promotion	Work diligently. Keep strong communication. Do not indulge in backstabbing or vilifying others in order to gain for yourself.	NV –Ahimsa is broken by contempt toward co-workers or even by entertaining dislike/prejudice toward them.
Sharing	Do not hide/withhold any information from others with the intention of using it for your own benefit.	NP – Not just possessions, but not sharing and "hoarding" ideas and information is possessiveness. Renounce with your heart.
Dealing with Vendors / Investors	Be honest in your dealings. Do not try to cheat by giving wrong information for your own/firm's profit.	NV – Be honest.

Tools/ Situations	My Actions	Core Values
Boss	Just because a person is your boss, do not endorse dishonest behavior.	NV
Mindfulness	Work with mindfulness, enthusiasm, energy, and determination.	NV – Be honest to your responsibilities.
Competition	Respect competitors and compete keeping core values in mind.	NP – Profits are good but not by denigrating your competitors.
Balance	Prioritize how your time and energy are spent in the workplace. If you're overworking, reconsider the situations.	NA – See things from work, home, family perspective.
Customers	Be forthright and straightforward. Do not exaggerate your claims.	NV – Tell the truth.

Jain Way of Life is making it a priority to provide for your family and making the world a better place through your company's products and services. Constantly expand your professional and personal skills.

The job market is competitive with fewer chances for promotions. However, there will always be opportunities for those who are recognized as having special talents and excelling at what they do. Practicing your core values is the most efficient way to move ahead in today's world. If you tap into your innate strengths and talents, you'll find that you'll excel much easier in the world of work.

"All human beings are miserable due to their own faults, and they themselves can be happy by correcting these faults." — Mahävir

Contributor: Anita Jain

Jain Relaxation and Meditation

Jain scriptures offer extensive guidance on meditation techniques to achieve full knowledge and awareness. Meditation is one of the most pleasant, serene, and joyous feelings. We can gain tremendous energy by managing our fickle mind. It offers us tremendous physical and mental benefits. The following table describes a simple, six-stage technique which you can use for yourself or to guide a family or group meditation session.

10 Minute Group or Individual Body Relaxation and Meditation:

Stages	What to Do	What to Say (to yourself or to a group you are guiding)	Notes and Options
Start: Breathing	Close your eyes, keep your back straight, and relax. Take three deep breaths: (count) Inhale, 2, 3, 4 – Hold, 2, 3, 4, Exhale 2, 3, 4, 5, 6 Inhale, 2, 3, 4 – Hold, 2, 3, 4, Exhale 2, 3, 4, 5, 6 Inhale, 2, 3, 4 – Hold, 2, 3, 4, Exhale 2, 3, 4, 5, 6	*First we'll relax the body, then relax the mind; let the full energy flow through your spine.* Take a deep breath. Make a nice strong sound. Let all the negativity out.	When inhaling, stomach should come out (because your diaphragm pushes down and your lung capacity expands). Be sure your chest is not expanding while inhaling.

Stages	What to Do	What to Say	Notes and Options
Body Relaxation	**Toes:** Move your toes around; stretch your **leg muscles**, and your **thigh muscles**. Stretch your **fingers** out wide, and bring them in; rotate your **wrist** in one direction, and then in the other direction. Raise your **shoulders** to your ears and down (3x). Bring your **chin** to your chest and head all the way back slowly. Feel the stretch. With your **right ear,** touch your right shoulder. Head back, left ear touch your left shoulder, and chin to your chest, (do this 3x) and reverse direction; Open your **mouth** wide, close (2x). Raise your **eyebrows** and close your **eyes** tightly. Take a deep breath. Relax.	Let's relax the body. Release some of the tension in the muscles. Relax the facial muscles.	Keep your eyes closed, back straight. Do it gently ... relax, think about which muscles you are relaxing, feel the tension leaving. Many muscles here; need to relax them.
Mind Relaxation	Keep your eyes closed; observe your breathing. Slowly observe your mind... see the thoughts... observe your thoughts. Gently escort your thoughts out. Don't get upset at yourself.	Now that the body is relaxed, we'll relax the mind. Keep your eyes closed.	(1) The mind is like a monkey running around in a cage... moves from one thought to another... like a stormy ocean... many thoughts arise. And as you go deeper and deeper in meditation, the ripples become smaller and smaller. (2) Focus on your breathing. Feel the cool air as it enters your nostrils, goes into every part of your body, and as you exhale all negative thoughts and energy are exhaled.

Stages	What to Do	What to Say	Notes and Options
Meditate	**Topic 1: Body/Soul** Meditate on: I'm the body and the Soul; The Soul is the real me and is eternal and divine but full of negative Karmic bondages. As I'm meditating, I'm getting stronger and many of the Karmas are getting weaker ... the bonds are getting weaker. They cannot influence me as my will power is getting stronger.	Now that the mind is relaxed, we will go deeper in our meditation.	See below for more topic ideas.
Silence	Meditate on the subject. Go deep on the subject.	Keep your back straight, keep you mind focused.	
End Session: Say a Mantra	In your mind, say namokar mantra, then on your lips and then all together: Inhale – (stomach out) say Ooooooooooooomm while exhaling Inhale – Ooooooooooooommmm Inhale – Ooooooooooooommmm	Now we'll end the session with three Namokar Mantras: once in the mind; once on the lips; and once together.	Think of the meaning of Namokar Mantra when chanting. (Bow to the Arihants – Siddhas – Āchārya – Upadhyas, and all Sädhus.)

You may ask yourself or the group about their meditation experience, or ask how the meditation was and get them to give a one minute guided meditation.

Guided Meditation Topics

The following are some sample topics on which to meditate. You can get some of these topics from scriptures or make your own topics.

Topic 1: Body/Soul Meditate on (and say it out loud) I'm the body and the Soul; The Soul is the real me and is eternal and divine, full of karmic bondages. And as I'm meditating, I'm getting stronger and many of the Karmic bondages are getting weaker ... bonds are getting weaker ... they cannot influence me as my willpower is getting stronger.

Topic 2: Out of Body experience Meditate on (and say it out loud) observe yourself sitting in this posture; see from the top of the room, school (or house where you are doing the meditation), town, state, country, world. Now imagine you are in outer space passing the planets, the solar system, the galaxy, and the Earth which is just a tiny tiny spec of this vast universe. You are free, eternal; you have infinite perception, power. Your Soul has infinite energy, infinite potential. Slowly, let's make our way back. We head toward Earth, pass the galaxies, pass the planets, and see our world from the top, [pause to appreciate the beauty of our planet Earth], see our country, our state, our town, our home, and observe ourselves from the top of the ceiling.

Topic 3: Sameru Parvat (mountain where Jain Tirthankars meditated) Meditate out loud that we are on top of the mountain. The clouds are dark and the mountain (Parvat) is surrounded by an angry, violent ocean. There is a huge storm. It is violently raining and thundering. The outside tumultuous ocean and clouds reflect your mind. As you go deeper in your meditation, the ocean waves become calmer. The clouds move out. You begin to see the light. A small beam of white light, full of energy spraying you as you are meditating. You go deeper in your meditation. Slowly the clouds move out, the thunder stops, the ocean is serene, and you are immersed in the beautiful white light. You are full of energy.

Meditation in Jain Scriptures[8]

Aayaro is the oldest Ägam of Jainism. It defines one who meditates as one who always knows the reality of the body's every moment. Described is another type of meditation called "Dristiwad." This meditation is to experience within oneself "as it is" and not as it appears or seems.

Vipasana is one of the techniques of meditation. Although this technique is in the tradition of Lord Buddha, it teaches yourself to remain apart from clinging and hatred (Raga and Dwesh) and to be liberated from all Karmas/bondages through Right Perception (Samyak Darshan), Right Knowledge (Samyak Jnän) and Right Conduct (Samyak Charitra).

Jain texts particularly describe the removal of Rag and Dwesh (clinging hatred), keeping Samta (equanimity) and awareness through meditation. Most Jain practice of meditation is in the form of Samayik and Pratikraman.

Add Meditation to Your Daily Life
- Do it for at least a few minutes a day.
- At temple and festival celebrations, divide up the prayer time such that meditation is done for 20% of the time.
- When going to bed, take a few minutes to meditate.
- While at a stop light, take a deep breath and meditate.
- Take a moment to meditate before starting a meal.

"A person who meditates for two and a half minutes purifying the mind surpasses one who has done a penance of fasting for two days. The power of meditation is infinite because a pure state of mind, consciousness is worth more than a thousand years of penance."
— Ächärya Mahaprajnaji

Meditation Guidelines by Yogendra Jain
8   http://www.nyjaincenter.org/meditation.aspx

My 12 Reflections

Humans have a great ability to mentally reflect on our current, past, and future. Jain scriptures eloquently prescribe 12 reflections to help us reinforce our Jain way of life practices. These reflections allow us to understand that we are alone in this world, but at the same time interconnected to every living being. By observing these reflections, we can deepen our view of Non-Violence, Non-Absolutism, and Non-Possessiveness.

#	Reflection	Description
1	Impermanence (*Anitya*)	I have come into this world alone and will leave this world alone. This world is impermanent. Everything is subject to change and transformation.
2	Inevitability of birth and death (*Asharan*)	Birth is inevitably followed by death. Kings and presidents with their powerful armies, scientists with their latest medical technology, and even gods cannot change this.
3	Wordly Existence (*Samsär*)	Worldly life is an ocean of illusion. No permanent relationships exist. The Soul moves from one body to another, one relationship to another, and can only exit this illusion through liberation.
4	Aloneness (*Ekatva*)	There is absolute solitude of each Soul. I am alone and responsible for my actions.
5	Separateness (*Anyatva*)	The world, my relations and friends, my body and mind, they are all distinct and separate from my real self. My real self, the Soul, is permanent.
6	Impureness (*Ashuchi*)	The body is impure and dirty. It transforms, changes and eventually turns to ashes. We must treat it with respect and care but not be attached to its external appearance.
7	Inflow (*Äsrav*)	Passions dominate our thoughts, speech and actions, and allow inflow of Karmas.

#	Reflection	Description
8	Stoppage (*Samvar*)	The inflow of negative and positive Karma can be stopped through meditation and, will power and knowledge.
9	Shedding (*Nirjarä*)	By shedding the negative as well as positive Karmas, we can liberate our Soul.
10	Universe (*Lokasvarup*)	The universe is vast and is in a constant state of flux. Compared to the vastness of the universe, our physical space and time is tiny.
11	Unattainability (*Bodhi Durlabh*)	It is difficult to attain Right Perception, Right Knowledge and Right Conduct; it requires proactive and mindful efforts.
12	Teachings of Arihants (*Dharma*)	Arihants, the monks who have attained complete knowledge, have shown us the path of Non-Violence, Non-Absolutism, and Non-Possessiveness.

These twelve Anuprekshas are meditations or reflections and have to be meditated upon again and again. Sometimes these Anuprekshas are termed as Bhävanäs (thoughts).

Bhävanä: (Contemplations)

The Jain Way of Life is about managing and balancing one's passion. Mindful Bhävanä (contemplations, yearnings, thoughts, aspirations, or reflections) can help us. These 12 Bhävanäs describe the subject of one's contemplations, and how to occupy one's mind with useful, religious, beneficial, peaceful, harmless, spiritually advancing, Karma-preventing thoughts. The Bhävanäs, also called Anuprekshas, help one to remain on the right course in life, and not to stray away. The person's daily behavior, practical life or action is the resultant of his internal thoughts.

1. Anitya bhävanä: The impermanence of the sansär or world

Nothing in the universe has permanence, even though the whole universe is constant. Spiritual values are therefore worth striving for as they alone offer the Soul, its ultimate freedom and stability.

2. Asharan bhävanä: The refuge to the sansär, i.e. world of becoming, is misleading

The Soul is in its own refuge, and to achieve total freedom and enlightenment to the true path, one takes refuge in teachings of Arihanta (have total knowledge), Siddha (liberated Soul), Aachärya (head of religious order), Upädhyäya (teachers) and Sädhus (monks and nuns). The refuge to things other than above due to delusion, is unfortunate, and must be avoided.

3. Samsär bhävanä: The worldly existence

The Soul transmigrates from one life to the other in four gatis (human, animal, hellish, heavenly) and is full of pain and miseries. The Soul must achieve ultimate freedom, which is moksha.

4. Ekatva bhävanä: The aloneness of the Soul

The Soul is solitary, and lonely in existence. The Soul assumes birth alone, and departs alone from the life form. It will be responsible for its own actions and Karmas. The Soul will enjoy the fruit as well as suffer bad consequences of its own action alone.

5. Anyatva bhävanä: The self-dependence, separateness

In this world one should be self-dependent. The Soul therefore should not develop attachment for worldly objects and beings.

6. Ashuchi bhävanä: The impureness of the body

The composition of the body will reveal all the things we loathe, such as excrement, urine, blood, meat, bones, sweat, and so on, and therefore is impure. The Soul, within the body but unattached to the body, alone is pure. The body ultimately becomes nonexistent, but the Soul continues on; it is eternal. Emotional attachment to the body is useless.

7. Äsrav bhävanä: Influx of Karma contemplations

Raag, Dwesh, ignorance etc. attracts new Karmas. Deluded state, and how to be free from delusion is the subject matter of this thought activity.

8. Samvar bhävanä: Stoppage of influx of Karma

To get absorbed in achieving spiritual knowledge, meditation prevents the influx of Karmas.

9. Nirjarä bhävanä: Karma shedding

The efficacy of discipline and penance for freeing oneself from the bondage of the Karma.

10. Lokasvarup bhävanä: Universe

To think of the nature and structure of the universe. The universe consists of six substances: Soul, Matter, Medium of Motion, Medium of Rest, Space, and Time.

11. Bodhidurlabh bhçvanä: Unobtainability of true talent

It is very difficult for the transmigrating Soul in this world (sansär) to develop Right Perception, Right Knowledge, and Right Conduct. So when you have the opportunity to learn Jain principles, take advantage of it to develop right religious talent.

12. Dharmadurlabh bhävanä: Unobtainability of true preceptor, scripture and religion

To be able to distinguish right religion, scripture, preceptor etc. from the wrong and to follow the right requires good judgment. The Dharma is characterized by:

Uttam (Right), Kshamä (Forbearance, Forgiveness), Uttam Mardava (Modesty, Humility), Uttam Arjav (Straightforwardness), Uttam Shauch (Purity), Uttam Satya (Truth), Uttam Sanyam (Self-restraint, Control of Senses), Uttam Tapa (Austerity, Penance), Uttam Tyaaga (Renunciation), Uttam Akinchanya (Non attachment), Uttam Brahmacharya (Celibacy, Chastity).

"Fight with yourself, why fight with external foes? He who conquers himself through himself will obtain happiness." — Mahävir

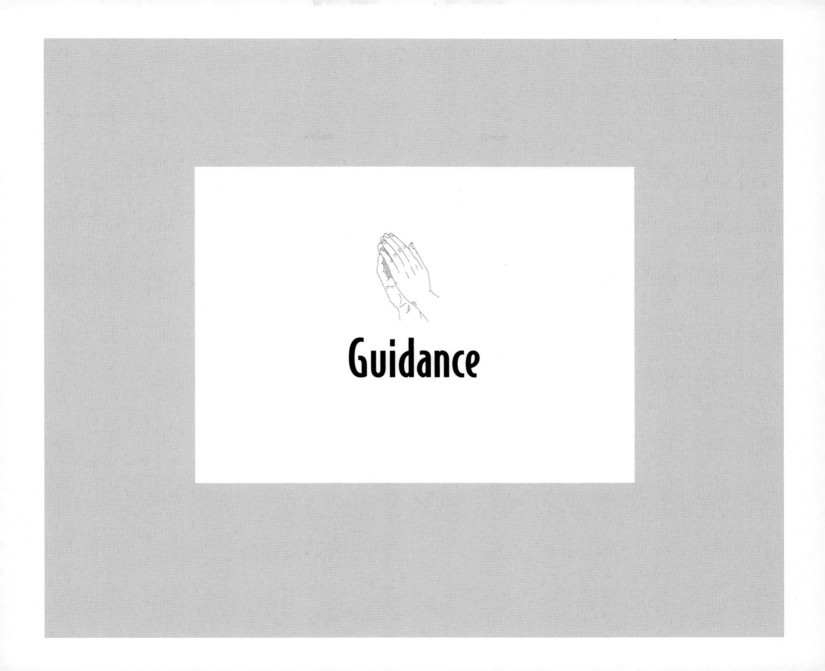

Guidance

Cherish the Jain Experience in North America

For Students, Visitors, Professionals, Family

Welcome to the United States of America. Whether you are a student, parent (visiting to help your son or daughter have their first child), on a temporary work assignment, or just visiting this country for vacation, it is very easy to maintain your Jain Way of Life practices. In fact, in North America you will experience new and innovative Jain practices and expand your understanding of this healthy and compassionate way of life.

North American Jains are dynamic and active with more than 68 Jain organizations and more than 30 Jain temples. All major Jain festivals are celebrated, and conventions are held every year for youths and families.

Caution: Jains in North America strive for unity among the various sects (Shvetämbar, Digambar, Sthanakvasi, etc.). Please bring your best practices from India and do not create sectarianism. Know that Jain traditions are rich and varied, and conducted in different languages with different idol images. Only by embracing these will you be practicing true Non-Absolutism (Anekantvad – multifacetedness). We want North American Jains now and in the future to practice and maintain their respective traditions and live as unified Jains practicing JWOL.

The following are some recommendations and guidelines

Restaurant	At restaurants, ask the server, "*What vegetarian items do you have on your menu. We don't eat meat, fish, eggs...*" Check the menu. Indian food: Naans have eggs in them. If you are eating a buffet, ask them to make roti for you. Thai: watch out for oyster or fish sauce in curry, eggs in pad thai. Italian: eggs in some types of pastas. Mexican: sometimes the beans are cooked in lard. Ice cream and dessert: watch out for eggs and gelatin.
Fast food	Always politely request them to change gloves, wipe the counter, and use a fresh knife at places like Subway, Quiznos, Pizza, Deli, Blimpies (and explain your reason ... "*I am a vegetarian*").

Drinking	There is absolutely no stigma in refraining from drinking alcohol. Even taking a sip or two is not necessary when making a toast. If you do want a nice tasty drink from the bar, you can always ask for virgin (non-alcoholic) drinks (such as Pina Colada, Strawberry Daquri, Margarita, etc.). Ask the waiter, *"What non-alcoholic drinks do you have?"* Do not give in to peer pressure.
Take a sip	When someone is asking you to take a sip, let them know "*I don't drink alcohol"* (and if it requires further explanation, *"I believe in Non-Violence in thoughts, words, and actions; and by drinking this drink my thinking will be impaired and I may say hurtful words or drive while drunk").*
Tipping	15%-20%. This is a must (even if you are a student) for service as the waiting staff expects this for part of their income. Thank them if they went out of their way to help you select delicious vegetarian options.
Indian Stores	Most cities have Indian stores. These stores carry a great variety of vegetarian foods and prepacked curries, sabjies and roti. Read the ingredients and know what they mean.
Jain Temple	Almost every major city has a temple. As you visit sites of major cities, take the time to visit Jain temples. All Jain temples have their web sites, locating them is easy (see Appendix on Jain Centers and Organization on page 178).
Driving	Politeness and safe defensive driving is key. Always be cautious. If in doubt to who has the right of way, let others through. Avoid using cell phone irresponsibly.
Purchasing	North America has liberal laws for returning purchases. If you discover any food item has an animal product in it, don't hesitate to return it. Also, please don't abuse this right by using a product and then returning it.
Honesty	Almost every person in North America is honest, respectful, and sincere.
Religious Celebrations	Every Jain center has a web site. Most Jain festivals celebrated in India are celebrated in temples across North America. Every Jain center conducts Pooja (prayers) and Pathshala (religious school) on a weekly or bi-weekly basis; detailed schedules can be found on the web site.
Fitness	Join a yoga or meditation group, exercise and stay healthy. Some university fitness centers are free.
Politeness	People are extremely polite. *Sorry, Please,* and *Thank You* are commonly used words. *Excuse me* can be used to get someone's attention if you are looking for help.
4th of July	Each 4th of July there are large gatherings of Jains. There is a JAINA convention every other year and YJA (Young Jains of America) every other year as well. There is also YJP organization for professionals.

JAINA (Federation of Jain Association of North America) is an umbrella organization for all Jain Centers. It has many projects that you can be part of and has a convention once every two years during the July 4th week.

Vegetarian Group: Join the local vegetarian group. You will learn about new and innovative healthy food. See Resources chapter for web links.

Contributor: Metri Jain

Guidelines for High School Students

High school years are demanding. Jain Way of Life offers a strong foundation for you to grow. The following are some issues you will come across throughout your high school years.

Issue	Jain Way of Life Response	Why
Dissection in Biology Class	Avoid dissection if you have an option. The National Anti-Vivisection Society (NAVS) is an organization that promotes dissection alternatives. Year after year, millions of animals are sacrificed to demonstrate basic anatomy and physiology that could easily be taught by more humane means. NAVS has CD-ROMs, software, models, videos, and anatomical charts and books regarding dissection. Other reputable science suppliers, such as Science Kit® and Boreal® Laboratories, have also developed models and charts that can replace dissection in science curriculums.[9]	There are many non-animal alternatives to dissection that teach children about life processes far more effectively than cutting up an animal. Using a non-animal alternative provides the necessary learning experience while also teaching young people a healthy respect for all life. Dissection, on the other hand, conveys the message that life is cheap and expendable. — NAVS
Sharing and Learning Jain Way of Life	In your high school classes, take opportunities to do papers and present on Jain Way of Life topics. Ask your teacher if you can give a 10 minute talk on JWOL. However, do not forget Anekantvad: be understanding of all other viewpoints and read about other world religions.	Introduce your classmates to a faith that is Non-Violent and respects beliefs of others.

Issue	Jain Way of Life Response	Why
Festivals	Let your friends know about your Diwali, Mahāvir Jayanti, and Paryushan festivals.	This will let them appreciate your faith and they will learn another view.
"Do you want to go out with me" (dating)	*"Thanks – I would very much like to be your friend, but at this time my focus is on studies and school. I'm sure you understand."*	The goal is to firmly but sensitively and categorically say NO. By getting into a relationship, there will be much more mental pain for all involved. It will be distracting, your parents will not approve of it and it can lead to other serious negative consequences.
Exercise	Your body is young and growing. Nourish it with great care. Exercise.	A healthy body places far less burden on others and society. It allows for a strong mental discipline, keeps you energized, and strengthens your hormonal balance. A healthy body is an ideal medium for spiritual progress.
Lunch	Find out which foods are vegetarian (without eggs). Ask your food director to have more vegetarian options and label it with a V sign on the menu.	Besides you, there may be many other students who would prefer this but are too shy to ask.
Stress	Keep life in balance. Take on only activities that you can handle without being irritated, moody, and angry.	Stress causes a great deal of violence to oneself as well as to people around us.
Club	Start a vegetarian club and/or an animal rights club.	Besides you, there may be many other students who would prefer this but are too shy to ask.
"Take a sip" (alcohol)	There is absolutely no stigma in refraining from drinking. Even taking a sip or two is not necessary. When someone is asking you to take a sip, let them know firmly, but politely, that "I don't drink."	*"I believe in Non-Violence in thoughts, words, and actions; and by drinking this drink my thinking will be impaired and I may say hurtful words or drive while drunk."* Moreover, underage drinking is illegal. If you feel pressured, talk with your parents or a trusted adult. Do not drink with friends. Drinking for the first time can be dangerous because you may have alcohol allergies and you do not know your tolerance. Peer pressure can lead you to making decisions you will regret later.

Issue	Jain Way of Life Response	Why
Alcohol, Drugs	Say NO.	These are illegal, addictive, and can lead to a lifetime of pain and suffering for you, your body, your family, and your society. The amount of violence that you can potentially cause is tremendous.
Prom	If you decide to go to the prom, go with someone not as a date but as a friend. Go with an Indian friend (or non-Indian who your family is comfortable with) who you can have a nice time with but without any commitment or expectations. Get your parents involved in the process, seek their permission and guidance, and let them know ahead of time. Work with them in contacting your friend's family, etc.	Prom can be a lot of fun, but there are several situations that can make the experience a source of mental anguish. Thinking ahead and exercising good sense will help you avoid these pitfalls.
I'm a Jain	You will be asked many times, why do you believe in ... what is your religion, etc. Your response should be very simple: "I believe in Non-Violence. That is the reason I am a vegetarian. I believe in respecting other views and I believe in balancing my possessions so we can all share this planet."	
Parents	It is natural to feel disagreeable with your parents on many issues. Respect your parents, understand their view, and be polite.	You will realize when you pass your teenage years and when you are a parent yourself that there was enormous wisdom in your parents' views.

You can play an active role in promoting vegetarianism. For example, high school student Priyanka Jain was awarded a scholarship for her activities promoting vegetarianism and animal right causes for several years.[10] These activities included leadership participation in vegetarian society functions, work at animal shelters, serving the homeless, giving talks in high school on vegetarianism and Non-Violence, getting vegetarianism and Ahimsa topics included in syllabus, encouraging high school food service to serve healthy and vegetarian food, founding the Action for Animal Liberation club, coauthoring a book on "Vegetarian Book for Teens," cooking vegetarian items in cooking class, and hosting Indian Vegetarian Cooking TV shows.

---

[9] http://sciencekit.com/
[10] Vegetarian Journal, Issue 4, 2006
http://www.navs.org/

Animal Rights – Your Critical Role

Animal rights is the core of Jain practice. For thousands of years, Jains have been protecting all types of animal life from abuse, consumption, and neglect.

Animal Rights (Modern definition) A philosophical and political position that animals have inherent rights comparable to those of humans.

Forms of Protecting Animal Rights - Which is your view?

Utilitarian view by Peter Singer, who, along with animal rights activists, argued that the well-being of all sentient beings (conscious beings who feel pain, including animals) deserve equal consideration with that given to human beings.

- **Rights-based** approach by Tom argues that non-human animals, as "subjects-of-a-life," are bearers of rights like humans. He argues that, because the moral rights of humans are based on their possession of certain cognitive abilities, and because these abilities are also possessed by at least some non-human animals, such animals must have the same moral rights as humans.

- **Abolitionist view** by Gary Francione's work (Introduction to Animal Rights, et.al.) is based on the premise that if non-

human animals are considered to be property, then any rights they may be granted would be directly undermined by that property status. He points out that a call to equally consider the 'interests' of your property against your own interests is absurd. Without the basic right not to be treated as the property of humans, non-human animals have no rights whatsoever, he says.

Jain Definition of Animal Rights

"The Lords and Conquerors of the past, present and future, all say thus, declare thus, explain thus in unison: all breathing, existing, living, sentient creatures should not be slain, nor treated with violence, nor abused, nor tormented, nor driven away. This is the pure, unchangeable, eternal law, which the clever ones, who understand the world, have declared: among the zealous and the not zealous, among the faithful and the not faithful, among the not cruel and the cruel, among those who have worldly weakness and those who have not, among those who like social bonds and those who do not: That is the Law, that is so, that is here proclaimed."

— Acharanga Sutra (1:4:1-2)

History of Animal Rights

The animal rights movement in the United States dates back to the 1700s. The modern movement took force in the early 1970s, and was a movement created by philosophers, and in which they remain in the forefront. A group of Oxford philosophers began to question whether the moral status of non-human animals was necessarily inferior to that of human beings. One of the group's members was the psychologist Richard D. Ryder, who coined the term "specimens" to describe the assignment of value to the interests of beings on the basis of their membership of a particular species. The movement grew in the 1980s and 1990s and was joined by professional groups, including theologians, lawyers, physicians, psychologists, psychiatrists, veterinarians, pathologists, and former vivisectionists.

Animal Support Groups (Just few of the many)

Name	Focus / Philosophy	What you can do
PETA	"Animals are not ours to eat, wear, experiment on, or use for entertainment."	PETA's aggressive advertising does mental violence to humans to help prevent physical violence to animals. The media coverage (free) is often effective, but you must decide if you support this method.
Animal Aid	Peacefully campaign against all forms of animal abuse and promotes a cruelty-free lifestyle.	Donate and participate! This key word here is *"peacefully"*
Animal Liberation Front	Engage in direct action on behalf of animals, which includes removing animals from facilities, or sabotaging facilities in protest against the animal testing, fur, meat, egg, or dairy industries.	Perhaps this is a semi-violent approach.
Animal Rights Militia	Animal-rights activists willing to engage in direct action that might endanger human life.	This is violent, and Jains should find an alternative way to get the message across.
BUAV (British Union for the Abolition of Vivisection)	Goal is the complete abolition of all animal experiments through education, research, investigations, including undercover work in laboratories, political lobbying, and legal cases.	This is more focused on the legal work against animal experiments, involving research and investigations, so like PETA, it is aggressive advertising, but it is nonviolent and for a very good cause.
Great Ape Project	Calls for an extension of moral egalitarianism to encompass all great apes.	This is a specialized animal-rights movement, but definitely one that should receive attention.

Justice Department	The Animal Liberation Front does not use nonviolence in its efforts for animal rights. An idea was established that decided animal abusers had been warned long enough. ... "The time has come for abusers to have but a taste of the fear and anguish their victims suffer on a daily basis."	This is quite violent, not something Jains should get involved with.
SPEAK	British animal rights campaign that aims to end animal experimentation and vivisection in the UK. Its current focus is opposition to a new animal testing center being built by Oxford University.	While this has a good cause, intimidation, incitement and violence have accompanied the campaign, so Jains should steer clear.
SHAC (labeled as terrorist organization)	International animal rights campaign against Huntingdon Life Sciences (HLS), Europe's largest contract animal-testing laboratory as well as financial institutions that invest in HLS.	This organization has been known to condone violence, intimidation, and attacks on property. Jains should not support this group.
VIVA! (*Vegetarians' International Voice For Animals*)	Animal-rights based organization which promotes vegetarianism and veganism. It portrays factory farming as being cruel, environmentally damaging, and unhealthy, and campaigns against it.	This is a very good cause stressing the vegetarian way of life, and something Jains should help to promote and campaign.

Recommendation for Jains

- Donate 0.5% of your income to animal rights but also don't forget to donate to shelters for battered women, drug education programs, programs to help former addicts/criminals change their lives, stress education, etc. There are plethora of ways to encourage non-violence.

- Be involved (volunteer, be part of protests, write-in campaigns).

- Deeper analysis: look deeper into the organization: How are they spending their money? How they are promoting their cause etc., so that you are not helping a violent or extremely aggressive organization?

"Ahimsa is not merely non-participation in destructive activities; it principally manifests itself in constructive activities and service, which leads to the upward growth of man" — Ächärya Vinoba Bhave

Contributor: Asmi Sanghvi

Partnerships with Non-Jain Groups

Sharing Jain Principles

Jainism is not only a religion, but a way of life. Gandhi once said, "As soon as we lose the moral basis, we cease to be religious. There is no such thing as religion overriding morality. Man, for instance, cannot be untruthful, cruel or incontinent and claim to have God on his side." Thus, we should not only look inwards toward our Soul, but at the world around us.

Morality involves a sense of responsibility to various issues that face the world in which we live. We all have heard the phrase that no man is an island, but how much do we really do for others?

We don't need to be radical demonstrators to stand for what we believe in. It can be as easy as making ourselves more aware of the world around us and spreading the word to friends and family. Write a letter to our world leaders, clean up a local park, serve a meal to a stranger, volunteer, and donate a portion of your paycheck. Learn what it feels like to make a difference. We must invest in the future of our world. This is living a Jain Way of Life.

What Can I do Now?

Be aware of the activities of these groups	Example: Read about them when you see their names mentioned in the paper; open your mail and read their requests for donations.
Pick a few and participate in their activities	Example: Attend a Vegetarian Society function; help build a house with Habitat for Humanity.
Let your friends and family know about these groups	Example: Share your knowledge and discuss these issues at lunch with friends or around the dinner table.
Attend a seminar	Example: Register for an online or live seminar; go to their events.
Share Jain principles with these groups	Example: Give a talk at the Vegetarian Society function on Vegetarianism in Jain Way of Life.

| Invite them to Jain gatherings | Example: Invite someone from an Anti-Vivisection group to a temple gathering; bring in a speaker from an Interfaith group to a pathshala class. |

Here is a quick go-to guide for organizations with causes that are strongly aligned with Jain beliefs and principles of Non-Violence, Non-Absolutism, and Non-Possessiveness.

Organizations and their Missions – Giving Back

Organization	Their Mission	Your Involvement	Web site
Food for Life Global	Eliminating hunger in the world by providing those in need with vegetarian food	Donate money, devote time.	http://ffl.org/
Habitat for Humanity	Their goal is to eliminate homelessness in the world.	Many ways to donate money or volunteer your time and help build homes, locally, nationally, and abroad.	http://www.habitat.org/
Indicorps	This organization gives Indians around the world the chance to contribute in the progress of the country that defines their identity.	Donate money, devote time, suggest programs for involvement.	http://indicorps.org/
Organ Donation	Non-possessiveness is at the base of this one. Enhance the life of another at no cost to you.	Sign up to donate your organs.	http://www.organdonor.gov/
The Random Acts of Kindness Foundation	This foundation encourages society to inspire others and pay it forward.	This web site lists inspirational activities that even younger children can enjoy. The message is simple and touches the root of our religion: to do good and be good.	http://www.actsofkindness.org/

Organization	Their Mission	Your Involvement	Web site
Share and Care Foundation	Their goal is to enhance the quality of life for the underprivileged in India by supporting healthcare, education, and the upliftment of women and children.	Attend their fundraising events, volunteer your time, donate money.	http://shareandcare.org/

Human Rights

Organization	What they stand for	Involvement	Web site
Amnesty International	They aim to protect individuals wherever justice, freedom and equality are denied.	Their web site provides heaps of information regarding world issues where basic human rights are denied. Read and gain awareness, spread the word.	http://www.amnestyusa.org/
Save Darfur	They are raising awareness about the genocide occurring in Darfur and are working to bring an end to the atrocities.	Learn about the situation, tell your friends, attend Darfur-related events in your community.	http://www.savedarfur.org/

Individual Growth

Organization	What they stand for	Involvement	Web site
The Art of Living	They are dedicated to serving society by strengthening the individual.	They provide many workshops and seminars around the world for upliftment.	http://www.artofliving.org/

Organization	What they stand for	Involvement	Web site
Sarathi	This foundation focuses on the art of yoga and yogic philosophy.	The web site has valuable information on yoga and provides many useful discourses on benefits and practicing methods. Learn and pass on the knowledge.	http://www.sarathi.org/
Vipassana	Vipassana is a form of meditation that focuses on the deep interconnection between mind and body through discipline. It brings about a greater sense of mental peace and self control.	Attend the 10-day course and go deeper within yourself through guided self observation.	http://www.dhamma.org/

Animal Rights/Environmentalism

Organization	What they stand for	Involvement	Web site
The Humane Society of the United States	This organization stands against animal cruelty and injustice.	Make a donation, learn more about how to help this cause.	http://www.hsus.org
Mutts Comics	This is a comedy with a cause. The strip promotes kindness toward animals and the environment around us in a simple way.	This is a fun one, for young and old alike, to gain awareness about larger issues.	http://muttscomics.com/
The National Anti-Vivisection Society	They are working to abolish animal exploitation and promote a sense of respect for animal rights.	Membership provides people with knowledge of how to be a more animal-friendly consumer, along with updates on how to help relieve animal suffering.	http://www.navs.org

Organization	What they stand for	Involvement	Web site
People for the Ethical Treatment of Animals	They work to protect the rights of animals and prevent exploitation for human needs.	Become an animal friendly consumer, donate money, gain awareness of issues taking place in the world.	http://peta.org/
Save the Tiger Fund	They are working to stop the killing of tigers and allow them to roam freely in their natural habitats. Numerous such organizations exist for the protection of various endangered species.	Gain awareness, spread the word, donate money.	http://www.savethetigerfund.org
Vegetarian Society	This society promotes an understanding for a vegetarian lifestyle.	Become a more vegetarian friendly consumer, donate money.	http://www.vegsoc.org/
WWF (World Wildlife Fund for Nature)	Their aim is to promote a harmonious relationship between humans and the environment in which we live.	Donate money, devote time, learn about the issues that exist in our surroundings.	http://www.wwf.org http://www.wwfindia.org

Just like the organizations above, there are thousands of others that are doing tremendous service to humanity. Get to know them. Help them. Partner with them. Live and share the Jain Way of Life.

Parasparopagraho Jivanam – All Souls influence each other through service which may be favorable or unfavorable; they cannot live independently of one another; they must bear the karmic results individually; they create a common environment and live together in wealth and woe. — Tattvärtha-Sutra

Contributor: Asmi Singhvi

Forgiveness and How to do it

One key ingredient to happiness is unconditional forgiveness. It is critical in the practice of nonviolence and transforming our thoughts, speech, and actions to equanimity and harmony.

It is as important to ask for forgiveness as it is to forgive others. Asking for forgiveness is so essential that it is the central aspect of the Jain ritual Pratikraman. In Pratikraman, we ask for forgiveness from all levels and from of living beings. By asking for forgiveness, we lessen the attachment to that event or incident and avoid such actions in the future. By asking forgiveness, we learn and better ourselves.

Benefits of Forgiveness:

- It reduces anger, depression and stress.
- One becomes more hopeful, peaceful, compassionate, and confident.
- Our relationships grow stronger.

What is Your Level of Forgiveness?

	Levels of Forgiveness	What is your level?
Level 1	Ignorance	Think cruel thoughts toward people, objects, and situations.
Level 2	Grudge	Express ill thoughts and keep grudge for years.
Level 3	Forgive	Mentally forgive a person you despised or had fight or disagreement with. Ask for forgiveness.
Level 4	Proactive	Ask for forgiveness from a person you despise or had strong disagreement.
Level 5	Universal	Forgive people and ask for forgiveness from all living beings every moment.

Stages of Forgiveness

	Stage I – Preventive Forgiveness	Stage II – Passive Forgiveness	Stage III – Active Forgiveness
Description	Preventive forgiveness is based on the idea that if one doesn't feel animosity toward someone, he or she will not need to forgive.	Passive forgiveness stresses indifference. The other person is neither a friend nor an enemy.	Active forgiveness involves completely forgiving someone regardless of what they have done.
Example	You resolve disagreements immediately, clarify misunderstandings early on, abstain from having unrealistic expectations of others, and you do not get jealous.	Assume someone has hurt your feelings in some way. You were unable to prevent the situation, and you are unable to completely forgive the other person. You decide to not speak with the other person. However, you do not attempt revenge or speak ill of them. You are sympathetic and pray for them.	Assume someone has hurt you emotionally and physically. He or she truly hates you, and considers you as his or her enemy. You do not attempt revenge on the person, nor think ill of them. Rather, you love and care for them as if you two were friends.
How to do it	Be friendly toward everyone. Be honest with yourself and with others. Don't let your ego control your thoughts, speech, and actions.	Refrain from thoughts, speech, and actions of revenge. Be indifferent; neither negative, nor positive in your behavior toward the other person.	Be unaffected by other people's thoughts, speech and actions. Maintain your compassion toward others regardless of what they do to you.

The Top 10 Steps to Forgiveness by Diana Robinson[11]

For many people forgiveness is one of the hardest steps of all in our progress toward freedom of spirit. Yet it is essential. For as long as we are unable to forgive, we keep ourselves chained to the unforgiven. We give them rent-free space in our minds, emotional shackles on our hearts, and the right to torment us in the small hours of the night. When it is time to move on, but still too hard, try some or all of these steps. (Note that these steps are appropriate for events resulting from an ongoing adult relationship with anyone. They may not all be appropriate for the random act of violence from a stranger, nor for someone who was abused as a child or while in some other position of true helplessness.)

1. Understand that forgiving does not mean giving permission for the behavior to be repeated. It does not mean saying

Forgiveness Prayer

KHAMEMI SAVVE JIVA
We forgive all living beings,
SAVVE JIVA KHAMAN TUME
We seek pardon from all living beings,
MITTI ME SAVVA BHOOE SU
We are friendly towards all living beings,
VERAM MAJJHAM NA KENVI
We seek enmity with none,
MICHCHHAMI Dukkadam
And we ask for forgiveness from all.

that what was done was acceptable. Forgiveness is needed for behaviors that were not acceptable and that you should not allow to be repeated.

2. Recognize who is being hurt by your non-forgiveness. Does the other person burn with your anger, feel the knot in your stomach, experience the cycling and recycling of your thoughts as you re-experience the events in your mind? Do they stay awake as you rehearse in your mind what you would like to say or do to "punish" them? No, the pain is all yours.

3. Do not require to know 'why' as a prerequisite to forgiveness. Knowing why the behavior happened is unlikely to lessen the pain, because the pain came at a time when you did not know why. Occasionally there are times when knowing why makes forgiveness unnecessary, but they are rare. Don't count on it and don't count on even the perpetrator knowing why.

4. Make a list of what you need to forgive. What was actually done that caused your pain? Not what you felt, what was done.

5. Acknowledge your part. Were you honest about your hurt or did you hide the fact that the behavior hurt you? Did you seek peace by reassuring the perpetrator that it was all right? Did you stay when you could or should have left? If so, then you, too, have some responsibility. (Here you start to move away from being a victim.)

6. Make a list of what you gained from the relationship, whatever form of relationship it was. Looking back you may be focusing on the negatives, the hurts. Yet if they were repeated, you must have stayed to allow the repetition. You did not remove yourself. Why? There must have been some positives if you chose to stay around. What were they?

7. Write a letter to the person (no need to mail it). Acknowledge what you gained from the relationship, and express forgiveness for the hurt. Allow yourself to express all your feelings fully. Do not focus only on the hurt.

8. Create a ceremony in which you get rid of your lists and the letter, symbolizing the end of the link between you. You may choose to visualize placing them on a raft and watching it drift gently away down a river. You may prefer to burn them and scatter the ashes. You may invent some other form of ritualized separation.

9. Visualize the person you are forgiving being blessed by your forgiveness and, as a result, being freed from continuing the behavior that hurt you.

10. Now that you have freed yourself from the painful links and released the pain, feel yourself growing lighter and more joyous. Now you are free to move on with your life without that burden of bitterness. Do not look back in anger.

"Go not to the temple to ask for forgiveness for your sins, first forgive from your heart those who have sinned against you."
— Rabindranath Tagore

---

[11] Diana Robinson, Ph.D., Professional Life Coach, Writer, Editor, Counselor, www.choicecoach.com

Steps to Spiritual Progress

For centuries humans have sought guidance on how they can progress on their spiritual journey. The sages who authored the Jain scriptures Ratnakarand Shrävakachar have laid out a systematic 11 step plan, much like Stephen Covey's *Seven Habits* *of Highly Successful People*. The 11 steps, which are like the rungs of a ladder, are called Shrävaka-pratimä. They begin with intuition and awakening and lead up to an ascetic life.

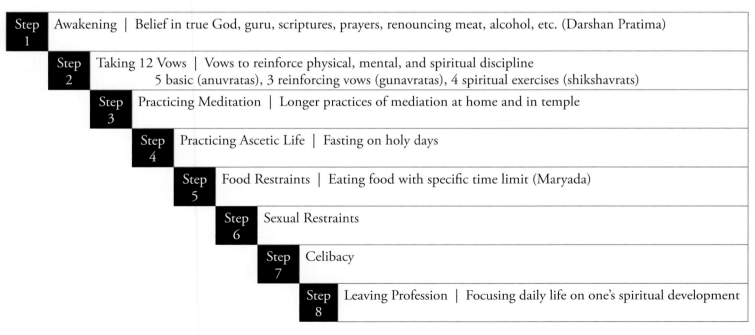

Step 1	Awakening | Belief in true God, guru, scriptures, prayers, renouncing meat, alcohol, etc. (Darshan Pratima)
Step 2	Taking 12 Vows | Vows to reinforce physical, mental, and spiritual discipline 5 basic (anuvratas), 3 reinforcing vows (gunavratas), 4 spiritual exercises (shikshavrats)
Step 3	Practicing Meditation | Longer practices of mediation at home and in temple
Step 4	Practicing Ascetic Life | Fasting on holy days
Step 5	Food Restraints | Eating food with specific time limit (Maryada)
Step 6	Sexual Restraints
Step 7	Celibacy
Step 8	Leaving Profession | Focusing daily life on one's spiritual development

Step 9	Leaving Possessions	Giving up possessions, money, as well as inner desire for these
Step 10	Family Detachment	Gradual detachment from family members and extended family and friends
Step 11	Leaving Family Ascetic Life	Leading an ascetic life and leaving family and home

14 Stages of Spiritual Development for Ascetics (Gunsāsthana)

In addition to these 11 steps, Jain Scriptures also outline the 14 stages of spiritual development known as Gunasthāna. These Gunasthāna as a progress metrics are more applicable for asectics and are specifically focused on the progress of the Soul from the impure state (bonded to many karmas) to the pure state of liberation (shedding of all Karmas). These 14 stages of spiritual develoment are:

Lowest stage: *1)* Stage of false beliefs with intense passion (*Mithyä-drashti Gunasthana*).

2) The stage of having tasted the righteousness (*Säsvadäna Samyak-drashti*).

3) Stage of fluctuation between the false and right belief (*Samyak-Mithyä-drashti*).

4) The stage of the right belief but no renunciation (*Avirata-Samyak-drashti*).

5) The stage of the right belief with the partial renunciation(*Desh-virat*).

6) The stage of the total renunciation (*Pramatta Samyati*).

7) The stage of the total renunciation and no carelessness (*Apramatta Samyat*).

8) The stage of an extraordinary effort (*Nivritti-Badar*).

9) The stage of almost passionless state (*Anivritti-Bädara*).

10) The stage of the subtle greed (*Sukshma-Samparäy*).

11) The stage of the passionless state by the suppression (*Upashänt-moha Kashaya*).

12) The passionless stage (*Kshina-moha*).

13) The stage of the omniscient with activities (*Sayogi kevali*)

Highest: *14)* The stage of the omniscient without activities (*Ayogi kevali*).

"I adore so greatly the principles of the Jain religion, that I would like to be reborn in a Jain community." — George Bernard Shaw

Celebrations

Family Celebrations

Birthday, Graduation, Mothers/Fathers Day, Anniversary, Marriage, Baby Shower

A Checklist

_____ Prayers – On the day of the celebration, contemplate on the event for a few minutes. Do longer prayers in the morning when you get up and before you go to bed.

_____ Family – Touch your parents feet or call them up and spend more time with them on the phone.

_____ Family – Call and/or visit your parents/grandparents and pay respect to them.

_____ Expectations – If your family, relatives, friends (or even your spouse) forgets this date, gently remind them without sarcasm and don't hold grudges.

_____ Temple – Try to go to temple on that day or on the weekend after the birthday, graduation, or anniversary.

_____ Party – If you are having a party at your home, be sure to have eggless cake.

_____ Party – If you are going to eat out or cater, try to go to a vegetarian restaurant or a place that has plenty of vegetarian food. If you are paying, then you should pre-order only vegetarian health food. Alcohol should not be part of any celebrations.

_____ On these auspicious days, make one resolution for the next year.

_____ Gifts I – Only accept gifts that are non-leather, silk, and non-animal tested. Mention this on the invitation card.

_____ Invitation Card – Instead of accepting gifts, let your guest know that NO gifts are accepted – but optionally you can ask them to donate to a charity that protects animals (Beauty without Cruelty, PETA, etc.) (See below.)

_____ Donation – Give a donation at the temple (Appx. 10% of the amount that you receive in gifts).

_____ Exercise – On celebration days, make it a point to celebrate your wonderful body. Exercise, meditate, pray, and relax.

_____ Recycle – Recycle plates, glasses, bottles. In large multi-day gatherings, put names on cups/glasses. Avoid styrofoam.

Additional Checklist Items for Specific Celebration

_____	Graduation	– Send a thank you note to some of your most supportive teachers, tutors, religious school teachers and mentors. Let them know how much their time and energy has made this day possible.
_____	Graduation	– Donate some amount to your school over time.
_____	Baby Shower	– Make a donation in the newborn's name to your temple.
_____	Baby Shower	– Instead of just throwing a party, also do a prayer.
_____	Anniversary	– Spend quality time with your spouse and family.
_____	Anniversary	– Go to the temple together.

Weddings with Jain Way of Life Mindfullness

Cost	The tradition is that the parents pay for the wedding, and the girl's side generally has higher expenses. However, if in North America where the parents may have already spent a considerable amount in education, the couple – especially if they are settled with a job or a strong future – must pay a significant portion of the cost.
Donation	5%-10% of the wedding cost should be set aside to donation (local temple, JAINA, other charitable organization).
Gifts	No silk, leather, or animal tested products.
English Translation	Have English translation handouts of the ceremony. In the handout, have a small paragraph explaining Jain Way of Life.
Alcohol	Absolutely no alcohol, not even champagne for toasting, at any of the functions. No open bar.
Fire, Butter	Avoid large pujä/ceremony fires as they harms insects.
Vegan and Jain Food	Have provisions for vegan and Jain food. Label the food clearly for non-Jain/Indian guests.
Namokar Mantra	Start all functions with a prayer. Make the occassion spiritual as well. Visit the temple after a major ceremony. Have a pujä/temple function a week or so before the marriage.

Gift Ideas (in Balance with JWOL)

For Children:

- Inexpensive toys
- Non-violent video or computer games (only educational) (Pay attention to ratings like M for mature and E for everyone.)
- A Jain coloring book or spiritual reading material

For Adults:

- Non-leather belt, wallet, shoes, etc.
- Books on health, business management, etc.
- A recipe book for vegetarians, vegans
- Non-fur/leather coat
- Massage chair, coupon for massage, etc.
- Jain books

Food Items:

- Gift card to Trader Joe's, Whole foods
- A nice fruit and vegetable basket
- Cook someone a nice vegetarian meal

For Family:

- Just visiting and spending quality time with parents/grandparents easily surpasses most any gift.
- Trip to JAINA convention
- Trip to India
- Relaxation, meditation CDs
- Jain video and/or CD
- Subscription to Jain/vegetarian magazines
- Jain books. Indian cultural books.

"One who, even after knowing the whole universe, can remain unaffected and unattached is God." — Mahävir

The Art of Dying
Samlekhanä – Death Attained with Complete Tranquility

Death is simply a change in state. Just as one changes a house or changes their clothes, with death the Soul changes from one body to another. Death can happen anytime. Hence at any moment we must be ready for this, and if it happens at a moment's notice or drawn out over years, we must be ready. This readiness happens with the strong practice of Non-Violence, Non-Absolutism, and Non-Possessiveness in thoughts, speech, and actions. "From the point of view of absolute principle (Nischay Nay), death in fact is like our mother. Just like our worldly mother, death gives us rebirth. Death brings another life for us. Death takes us from one way to another way of life, from one body to another body. She is the giver of liberation (Moksha). She liberates us from the cycle of birth and rebirth."[12]

Death Readiness

Just as learning requires not just bookish knowledge but experience and contemplation on the subject, similarly we must contemplate and prepare for death. It is important that one makes their wishes known and legally executed.

Type of Death/ Stage of Life	Examples	What to do	Preparation
Sudden-immediate death	Car accident	Take a deep breath. Try your best to save yourself; Even if you have a few seconds to live, take the time to forgive and ask for forgiveness from all the people and living beings you may have hurt (Say Michhami Dukkadm); recite Namokar Mantra; take a deep breath.	You may have completed the paperwork for donation.
Imminent Death	Disease, you have less than six months to live	Confirm DNR orders (Do Not Resuscitate – see next page); Don't give up; take your medications; minimize the pain; stay mindful and mentally alert; embrace family visits; ask for forgiveness; mentally practice more and more non-possessiveness; take limited vows.	Donate your possessions; Sign up for organ donation; Review will and trust.

Type of Death/ Stage of Life	Examples	What to do	Preparation
Few years to live	Cancer or severe heart attack or in late stages of aging	DNR orders in place; see the world; go on a pilgrimage; volunteer your time; keep life in balance.	Review will and trust. Sign up for organ donation.
Retired	Had a nice career, now focus on other aspects of life	DNR orders in place; do spiritual reading (Swadhyay), contemplation, meditation; see the world; go on a pilgrimage; volunteer your time; keep life in balance.	Update will and trust. Sign up for organ donation.
30-60s	Busy with family, stress	Understand that death can come at any moment; live life in balance.	Sign up for organ donation; put DNR paperwork in place be careful as to the types of conditions you put in DNR
Teens and 20s	Healthy and growing; enjoying life	Understand that death can come at any moment; be sure you have appropriate life insurance.	Sign up for organ donation; put DNR paperwork in place.

Medical and Legal Preparation

(DNR) Do Not Resuscitate Orders At times it is much more painful to oneself and family if you request strong life sustaining heroic measures. Such measures, if successful, will lead to a life of extreme mental and physical inability. Also, under such conditions, you may place enormous burdens on your family, your spouse's finances, and on the medical system.[13]

This is an advance directive for your doctor in case you are unable to make medical decisions (for example, if you are in a coma). Each state has different laws. You can include advance directive in:

1) Living Will – This is a written legal document which outlines the life sustaining treatment you desire to have.

2) Durable Power of Attorney for Health Care – Here you choose a person to make your health care decisions if you

are unconscious or unable to make medical decisions.

3) DNR Order – This is a type of advance directive. You can request not to have CPR (cardiopulmonary resuscitation) if the heart stops or if you stop breathing.

Reflections (through life and near death)

- *I came in this world alone and I will die alone – that is the nature of human life.*

- *I love my family, friends, and this wonderful life; now it's time for me to detach myself from them and my possessions.*

- *Having a human life was a great opportunity. I will strive to take birth as a human again and grow even more spiritually.*

- *I must give up my negative passions of jealousy, anger, greed, ego, and deceit.*

Post Death – Practical Steps

The following is a guideline for celebrating death:

Select funeral home	Select one which offers cremation.
Inform	Call few friends and close family members and ask them to inform other relatives.
Dates	Decide on the date and time of the funeral with funeral home availability and arrival of key out of town relatives.
Email-Web Page	Send email to or put up a simple web site with dates, photos, etc. of the deceased person. Make the request that mourners **not bring any flowers**. If possible, place a web page up quickly with all the information.
Body preparation	Prepare body as guided by the funeral director.
Dressing the body	Dress the body conservatively.
Funeral	Have a funeral where you can fit expected number of people. Keep the ceremony simple and short.
Web Page	If possible, do a web page and highlight the values and accomplishments.
Cremations	Traditionally Jains cremate the body.
Ashes	Different families have different traditions on how to best dispose of the ashes. Collection and display of ashes or to disperse them in a river or take it back to your hometown is not necessary.
3rd Day	A prayer at home or temple marks the resumption of regular home, family, and work activities.
13th Day	Official mourning stops at this time and the family members go back to their normal activity including visiting the temple.

Samlekhanä (Spiritual Death)

The Jain tradition gives great importance to death and the process of dying, a spiritual and practical practice called Samlekhanä (also known as Santhärä or Samädhi Maran). It is prescribed equally for ascetics as well as lay followers. Samlekhanä is a process of dying by gradually withdrawing from eating food in such a manner as it would never disrupt one's inner peace and dispassionate mindfulness.

The art of living is normally prescribed by almost all religions, but Jainism goes a step further by teaching the art of dying. A Buddhist monk, Bhikshu Kashyap, once said, "I have learnt many things from Buddhism, but I have to learn the art of dying peacefully from Jainism." The same idea was also expressed by the Gandhian thinker, Vinoba Bhave, who actually practiced Samlekhanä.[13]

The word "Samlekhanä" consists of two words: "Sam" and

"Lekhanä." "Sam" means in the right way and "Lekhana" means to emasculate the physical body as well as the passions. Thus, "Samlekhanä" implies deliberate emasculation of the (karmic as well as gross physical) body and passions like anger, pride, deceit, and greed. It has been described in detail in Jain canons like Bhagavati Aradhana, Uttaradhyayana Sutra, etc.

When to do Samlekhana

Samlekhanä cannot be practiced arbitrarily. A healthy ascetic or a lay person who is competent to perform religious or other activities is not allowed to embark on this. This practice is recommended only when the body is completely disabled by extreme old age, incurable disease, or situations where the death is unavoidable and imminent. Unlike suicide which is a result of outburst of passion, a person undertaking Samlekhanä is calm, dispassionate, and mindful.

How to do Samlekhanä

There are two steps to the path of this spiritual dying.

Step 1: Renouncing Passions (Kashäy Samlekhana)– A person must first free himself of passions by practicing internal austerities, scriptural reading, getting guidance from monks/nuns, and meditation. Specifically, forgiving and asking for forgiveness from family, friends, acquaintances, and all living beings; renouncing all possessions including home, wealth, etc.; ending grief, fear, anguish; adopting five Mahävrata (Non-Violence, Truth, Non-Stealing, Celibacy, Non-Possessiveness)

Step 2: Emancipation of Body – Only after successfully completing the first step of renouncing passions is one ready for the final step. One slowly gives up solid food, then liquid, then water, and in the end observes total fasting with all determination. Throughout this process with help from spiritual teachers, friends, and family one is immersed in reciting prayers, listening to scriptures, and immersed in meditation when possible. With the focus on the Soul one dies peacefully and blissfully and abandons the body.

Duration of Samlekhanä

The duration of this process can range from minutes to years. For example, if one is near death, they can mentally go into a state of meditation and renounce passions (Step 1) and mentally ready themselves for emancipation of the body (Step 2). This can be done in minutes if death is imminent. For others who may be afflicted with incurable disease, and death is months away, they can start the Samlekhanä process gradually through limiting type of food, multistages of fasting, etc.

Samlekhanä in North America

The question is how to adopt Samlekhanä in our lives in North America where the medical, legal, and political systems are complex? One can follow Step 1 of Samlekhanä while undergoing life saving medical treatment and can refuse commencing or stop treatment which is ineffective and may further cause injury. Recently, Oregon legalized the **Death with Dignity Act**, the first jurisdiction in the world to have such a law. This legalizes a terminally ill patient to choose the time of their death through assistance of a physician by administering a lethal dose of medication. However, assistance from another individual or through lethal dose of medication is not considered Samlekhanä.

Samlekhanä Versus Suicide

Samlekhanä is completely opposite to suicide. The following table highlights the differences:

Suicide	Samlekhanä
Means killing oneself.	Means removing the attachment from the body by understanding the reality of nature.
Typically done in a fit of strong detachment and aversion as a result of a deluded mind. It is based on fear, desire, passion, and lust. One tries to give up life to escape from worldly troubles.	Is not aimed at ending one's life but it is done to attain purity of consciousness, which ultimately ends in self-realization. Samlekhanä is, therefore, called as Samadhi-marana, i.e. death attained with complete tranquility and equanimity. Such a person is not eager to meet death, but is willing to face death with grace and equanimity as it comes over the course of time. Is not taken in a fit of attachment or aversion, neither is it a result of delusion. If someone undertakes Samlekhanä to kill himself immediately due to physical disease or depression as a result of a problem, it is not considered Samlekhanä.
At the time of suicide, the physical body is overwhelmed with stress; death comes suddenly.	Death is a natural phenomenon. A person is fully relaxed.
The person commits suicide with the aid of poison, weapon or any other similar means. The aim of such activity is to end life suddenly.	A person gradually eases into death with mindfulness, preparedness, and guidance. Accepts death as an experience that the Soul goes through when it departs the body.
Can be done by anyone based on their mental condition.	The difficult path of Samlekhanä can be followed only by a spiritual aspirant who has practiced spiritualism thoroughly, who has experienced that the body and the Soul are totally different. The aspirant realizes that the body is temporary and lifeless while the Soul is permanent and the seat of consciousness and life.

"Know thyself, recognize thyself, be immersed by thyself – you will attain Godhood." — Mahävir

[12] "The Nature of Death" by Sujanmal Modi (Original Gujarati article)
[13] *Ansana – The Art Of Dying Peacefully*, by Samani Madhur Pragya; Jain Digest Summer 2006
[14] www.familydoctor.org/003.xml – more information on DNR and State Laws

Jain Festivals

Generally, festivals are celebrations and jubilations characterized by excitement, enthusiasm, enjoyment and entertainment; but the Jain festivals are characterized by both the external and internal celebration. This internal celebration is through renunciation, austerities, study of the scriptures, meditation, and expressing devotion for the Jinas (idols). Even those people who are caught in the meshes of mundane life, according to their ability and conveniences, get free from the external worldly entanglements to the extent possible and become immersed in worship and meditation.

Paryushan Das-Lakshan Mahaparva

The Paryushan is the most important festival among the Jain festivals. It is observed during every Chaturmas (rainy season during late August/September) commencing on the twelfth day of the fortnight of the waning moon, in Bhadrapad and ending on the fourteenth of the fortnight of the waxing moon in the Bhadrapad. During these eighteen days, the entire Jain Society becomes spellbound in an atmosphere of enthusiasm and felicity. Jains young and old perform tap, some perform Atthai Tap—fasting for eight/ten days at a time. Some men, women and even children also take the vow of various types. During these days, scholars and monks visit temples and explain Jain

philosophy so as to expand internal austerity of the Soul along with observance of external tapa (fasting, etc.). All the members of the congregation listen to that explanation, overwhelmed with the emotion of devotion. Seven days are days of attainment and the last day is the one of fulfillment or achievement. In this manner, the Samvatsari Mahaparva festival is celebrated. Das-Lakshan is observed for ten days. At the conclusion of Paryushan, Pratikraman is done for repentance of faults and forgiveness is given and asked for from all.

Mahävir Jayanti (Birth Celebration)

The birthday of Mahävir, the last Tirthankar, is celebrated on the thirteenth day of the fortnight of the waxing moon, in the month of Chaitra. On this occasion, a grand chariot procession, community worship, glorification of the Lord, discussions, discourses, seminars and devotional and spiritual activities are organized.

Diwali (Mahävir's Liberation)

Diwali is celebrated on the new-moon day of Kartik, usually in October/November. On the night of that day, Mahävirswami attained Nirvana or deliverance and attained liberation. The Lord discarded the body and the bondage of all Karmas on

that night at Pavapuri and attained Mukti or deliverance. These three days are celebrated with Paushadh, fasting, special repetition of holy hymns, and meditation. Some fast on the Chafurdasi (14th day) and the new-moon day and listen to the Uttaradhyayan Sutra, which contains the final message of Lord Mahävir. During the night of Diwali, holy hymns are recited and meditation is done on Mahävir. In the early morning of the first day of the new year, Ganadhar Gautam Swami, the first disciple of Lord Mahävir, attained absolute enlightenment. The Jains begin the new year with a glorification of Lord Gautam Swami, and listen with devotion to the nine Stotras holy hymns and to the auspicious Rasa (epical poem) of Gautam Swami.

Nav Pad Oli/Siddhachakra Pujä

Twice a year for 9 days starting from the 6/7th day in the bright fortnight until the full moon day in Ashvin and Chaitra months, one does Äyambil. These Äyambils can also be restricted to only one kind of food or grain per day, and all fatty, fried, spiced, green foods are avoided. Many avoid salt also. Siddhachakra pujä is also performed for nine auspicious elements (panch parmeshthi, darshan, gyän, chäritra and tap). This practice is associated with the story of Shripal and Mayana Sundari, who performed this austerity and pujä with samyak darshan.

Bhai Beej (Dooj) *The festival day for brothers*

When Raja Nandivardhan, the brother of Mahävir was steeped in sorrow and anguish on account of the latter's Nirvana (attainment of Mukti), his sister, Sudarshana, took him to her house and comforted him. This happened on the second day of the fortnight of the waxing moon in Kartik. This day is observed as Bhai Beej. This festival is like Rakshabandhan. On the day of Rakshabandhan, the sister goes to the brother and ties the Raksha; but on this day, the sister invites her brother to her house to felicitate him.

Gyän Panchami *The holy day for acquiring knowledge*

Gyän Panchami is the name given to the celebration that takes place on the fifth day of the fortnight of the waxing moon in Kartik (the fifth day after Diwali). This day is devoted for worship of pure knowledge, which includes worshipping and fasting. Also on this day books preserved in the religious libraries are cleansed and worshipped.

Ashadh Chaturdasi

The sacred commencement of Chaturmas (during rainy season in India) takes place on the 14th day of the fortnight of the waxing moon, in the month of Ashad. The Jain monks and nuns (Sädhus and Sädhvis) remain where they happen to be for four months until the 14th day of Kartik Shukla. During these four months the monks give daily discourses, undertake religious ceremonies, etc.

Kartik Poornima *The full moon day of Kartik*

The Chaturmas that begins on Ashadh Chaturdashi comes to an end on the full moon day in Kartik. After this, the Jain Sädhus and Sädhvis begin their wandering Padyatra, i.e., travel on foot. A pilgrimage to Shatrunjay-Palitana on this day is considered to be of great importance. Thousands of Jains go on pilgrimages on this day.

Maun Ekadashi *The holy day for observing silence.*

Maun Ekadashi falls on the 11th day of the fortnight of the waxing moon in the month of Margshirsh. This is an important day for Jains on which they observe total silence, Maun and carry out such austerities as Paushadh vrat, fasting, worshipping, meditation etc. This is the day on which the great events relating to the 150 Jineshvars are celebrated by means of holy recitation. The story of Suvrat Shresthi is connected with this day.

Pushya Dashami

This day is famous as the birthday of Bhagwan Parshwanath. On the 10th day of Pushya, Jain men and women perform the tapasya of 3 Upavas-attham (continuous fasting for 3 days)

and by means of recitation and meditation they try to attain spiritual welfare. Thousands of people gather here and perform the austerity of Attham.

Akshay Tritiya

Those noble people who perform the austerity of Varsitap complete the austerity on this day by taking sugarcane juice in the cool shadow of Shatrunjay. Bhagwan Rishabhdev performed the Parana (completion of an austerity) on this day after fasting for one year continuously. This day is considered to be very auspicious for going on a pilgrimage to Shatrunjay. This falls on the 3rd day of the bright fortnight of Vaishakh.

With the exception of Paryushan/Das-Lakshan, Mahavir Jayanti, and Diwali, the other festivals are not actively observed in North America. However, in living a Jain Way of Life, one should pause on these days to understand the meaning of these beautiful festivals.

Mahāvir's Life and Teachings, Mahāvir Jayanti and Diwali

Lord Mahāvir was the twenty-fourth and last Tirthankar of Jains in this era. According to Jain philosophy, all Tirthankars were human beings but they attained a state of perfection or enlightenment through meditation and self-realization. They are the Gods of Jains. Mahāvir rejected the concept of God as a creator, a protector, and a destroyer of the universe. He also denounced the worshiping of gods and goddesses as a means of material gains and personal benefits and God's abilities to absolve their believers from their sins.

Lord Mahāvir was born on the thirteenth day of rising moon of Chaitra month, about 2,600 years ago (599 B.C.) in Bihar, India. This day falls in the month of March/April as per the English calendar. His birthday is celebrated as **Mahāvir Jayanti** day. Mahāvir was a prince and was given the name Vardhaman by his parents. Being the son of a king, he had many worldly pleasures, comforts, and services at his command. But at the age of 30, he left his family and royal household, gave up his worldly possessions, and became a monk in search of an unconditional solution to eliminate pain, sorrow, and suffering.

Mahāvir spent the next twelve and half years in deep silence and meditation to conquer his desires, feelings, and attachments. He carefully avoided harming or annoying other living beings, including animals, birds, and plants. He also went without food for long periods. He was calm and peaceful against all unbearable hardships and was given the name Mahāvir, meaning very brave and courageous. During this period, his spiritual powers were developed and in the end he realized perfect perception, knowledge, power, and bliss. This realization is known as keval-jnän or the perfect enlightenment.

Mahāvir spent the next 30 years traveling bare foot around India, preaching to the people the eternal truth he realized. The ultimate objective of his teaching is how one can attain total freedom from the cycle of birth, life, pain, misery, and death, and achieve the permanent blissful state of one's self. This is also known as liberation, nirvana, absolute freedom, or Moksha.

Mahāvir explained that from eternity, every living being (Soul) is in bondage of karmic atoms that are accumulated by good or bad deeds. Under the influence of Karma, the Soul is habituated to seek pleasures in materialistic possessions. This deep rooted habit is the cause of self-centered violent thoughts, deeds, anger, hatred, greed, and such other vices. These result in further accumulation of Karmas.

Mahāvir preached that Right Perception (samyak-darshan), Right Knowledge (samyak-jnän), and Right Conduct (samyak-chāritra) together is the real path to attain the liberation of one's self. At the heart of Right Conduct for Jains lie the five great vows:

Five Great Vows

- **Non-Violence (Ahimsa)**: not to cause harm to any living beings
- **Truthfulness (Satya)**: to speak the harmless truth
- **Non-stealing (Astey)**: not to take anything not properly given
- **Chastity (Brahmacharya)**: not to indulge in sensual pleasure
- **Non-Possession/Non-Attachment (Aparigrah)**: complete detachment from people, places, and material things

Jains hold these vows at the center of their lives. These vows cannot be fully implemented without the acceptance of a philosophy of non-absolutism (Anekantvad) and the theory of relativity (Syadvad). Monks and nuns follow these vows strictly and totally (great vows), while the common people follow the vows partially (minor vows) as far as their lifestyles will permit. In the matters of spiritual advancement as envisioned by Mahāvir, both men and women are on equal footing. The lure of renunciation and liberation attracted women as well. Many women followed Mahāvir's path and renounced the world in search of ultimate happiness. Thus, the principles of Jainism, if properly understood in their right perspectives and faithfully adhered to, will bring contentment and inner happiness and joy in the present life. This will elevate the Soul in future reincarnations to a higher spiritual level, achieving perfect enlightenment, reaching its final destination of eternal bliss, and ending all cycles of birth and death.

Mahāvir attracted people from all walks of life, rich and poor, kings and commoners, men and women, princes and priests, touchable and untouchable. He organized his followers, into a fourfold order, namely monk (Sādhu), nun (Sādhvi), layman (Shrāvak), and laywoman (Shrāvika). This order is known as Jain Sangh. Lord Mahāvir's sermons were orally compiled by his immediate disciples in Āgam Sutras. These Āgam Sutras were orally passed on to the future generations. Over the course of time, many of the Āgam Sutras have been lost, destroyed, or modified. About 1,000 years after Mahāvir, the Āgam Sutras were recorded on Tadpatris (leafy paper that was used in those days to preserve records for future references). Shvetāmbar Jains have accepted these Sutras as authentic versions of his teachings while Digambar Jains use them as a reference.

At the age of 72 (527 B.C.), Lord Mahāvir attained Nirvana and his purified Soul left his body and achieved complete liberation. He became a Siddha, a pure consciousness, a liberated Soul, living forever in a state of complete bliss. On the night of his Nirvana, people celebrated the Festival of Lights (Dipavali) in his honor. This is the last day of the Hindu and Jain calendar year and is known as **Diwali** (festival of lights) or **Deepavali** (meaning string of lights).

Jainism existed before Mahāvir, and his teachings were based on those of his predecessors. Thus, unlike Buddha, Mahāvir was more of a reformer and propagator of an existing religious order than the founder of a new faith. He followed the well established creed of his predecessor Tirthankar Parshvanāth. However, Mahāvir did reorganize the philosophical tenets of Jainism to correspond to his times.

A few centuries after Mahāvir's nirvana, the Jain religious order (Sangha) grew more and more complex.

Mahāvir's Simple Message

Mahāvir made religion simple and natural, free from elaborate ritual complexities. His teachings reflected the internal beauty and harmony of the Soul. Mahāvir taught the idea of supremacy of human life and stressed the

LIVE AND LET LIVE

importance of the positive attitude of life. Mahāvir's message of Non-Violence (Ahimsa), Truth (Satya), Non-Stealing (Achaurya), Celibacy (Brahmacharya), and Non-Possession (Aparigraha) is full of universal compassion. He said that, "A living body is not merely an integration of limbs and flesh but it is the abode of the Soul which potentially has perfect perception (Anant-darshan), perfect knowledge (Anant-jnän), perfect power (Anant-virya), and perfect bliss (Anant-sukh). Mahāvir's message reflects freedom and spiritual joy of the living being. Mahāvir emphasized that all living beings, irrespective of their size, shape, form, how spiritually developed or undeveloped, are equal and we should love and respect them. This way he preached the gospel of universal love.

Mahāvir Jayanti (Birth) and Liberation (Nirvan) Celebration

Jains across the world celebrate Mahāvir's birth and liberation. In North America, the celebrations are as follows:

1. Let your friends and family members know that Mahāvir Jayanti is approaching and family and community plans to celebrate it.

2. Plan the Mahāvir Jayanti day such that you can go to work late that day or take a holiday.

On Mahāvir Jayanti Day

1. Go to the temple if possible.

2. Do one hour of Abhishek (traditional bath) of Mahāvir image, prayers and pujā (Namokar Mantra, Mahāvir pujā, etc.)

3. Read to the family Mahāvir's message and his life story and meditate on his message.

4. Let people in your work and school know the significance of this day.

At Temple Functions

1. Let the young kids give a talk on the life story of Mahāvir.

2. Invite guest speakers to this event.

3. Participate in the exhibition of the Mother Trishla's (Mahāvir's mother) 14 or 16 dreams and help the temple and community to raise funds.

4. Dinner celebration.

In India, Mahāvir Jayanti is Celebrated as Follows:

• Temples that host Mahāvir Jayanti festivals are decorated with flags to mark the birthday of Lord Mahāvir.

• Each locality holds a traditional bath (*abhishek*) for an idol of Lord Mahāvir.

• Following the bath, the idol is carried in a procession throughout the region.

• Depending on the region, the parade ends at a temple, shrine or large communal area where people may pray and meditate.

• Donations made during Mahāvir Jayanti are made in the form of food, medicines or knowledge.

"Jainism believes in the plurality and equality of all living creatures. Since nobody wants to be hurt or killed, the general rule should be that nobody should be hurt or killed. This is the essence of Ahimsa. Absence of violence of all sort toward all beings at all times is Ahimsa." — Yogasutra

Source: Lord Mahāvir and His Teachings, compiled by Pravin Shah

Celebration of the Soul
Paryushan Parv and Das Lakshan

Paryushan is an eternal festival relating neither to people nor to any historical event. It is a time to celebrate the natural qualities of the Soul. Just as the Soul does not have a beginning or an end, Paryushan does not have a beginning or an end. It falls three times a year but is only celebrated once, around August/September because at this time, business is slow (in India), businessmen can take time off for spiritual pursuit. Also, it is the time of the monsoon retreat for monks and nuns in India. During this time when insects flourish, the monks and nuns reside in one city or community to avoid long distance travel so as to minimize trampling or harming living beings.

Eating, drinking and being merry are normally associated with festivals, but Paryushan is the festival for spiritual upliftment. During Paryushan, Jains practice penances, vows, fasts, scriptural studies, and Pratikraman. If not fasting, they refrain from eating green vegetables. The reason for these practices is to have the mind and body focus more on the inner qualities and virtues of the Soul and cleanse the body.

In North America, there are 18 days of celebration, in which the first 8 days are Paruyshan Parv celebration and the next 10 days are Das Lakshan (Festival of the Ten Virtues) celebration. After the celebration, Jains ask for forgiveness from each other,

their friends, co-workers, and most importantly, their enemies. This asking for forgiveness is made easier after the 8/10/18 days of cleansing of our Mind and Soul such that our hearts become "soft" and we become mentally strong to ask for forgiveness. First we forgive others, and then we ask for forgiveness.

Ten Supreme Dharmas (Das Lakshan)

The ten Dharmas, as also described in Tattvarth Sutra, are better understood in context of two common viewpoints found in the scriptures.

Vyavahar (External) view This view helps us live more easily and peacefully with the outside world. It also builds up a reserve of good deeds (punya Karmas). In Jainism, the Vyavahar view is considered a temporary view and a path towards Nischay view.

Nischay (Internal) view This view helps to enhance and blossom the Soul's natural qualities. The Nischay view is considered to be the most important as it leads to contemplation and understanding of the true nature of the Soul with the aim of its purification, the ultimate goal of practicing Paryushan.

Each of the ten Dharmas are all prefixed by the word 'Uttam' (Supreme) to signify that they are practiced at the highest level by the Jain monks. The householder practices them to a lesser extent. It lasts over a period of ten days, each day being dedicated to one of the ten Dharmas. These Dharmas are outlined below from both External View (Vyavahar View) and Internal View (Nischay) View.

1) Forgiveness – UTTAM KSHAMA

External View: We forgive those who have wronged us and seek forgiveness from them. Forgiveness is sought not just from human colleagues, but from all living beings ranging from one sense to five senses. If we do not forgive or seek forgiveness but instead harbor resentment, we bring misery and unhappiness on ourselves and in the process shatter our peace of mind and make enemies. Forgiving and seeking forgiveness oils the wheel of life, allowing us to live in harmony with our fellow beings.

Internal View: Forgiveness here is directed toward oneself. The Soul, in a state of mistaken identity or false belief, assumes that it consists of the body, the Karmas and the emotions, likes, dislikes, anger, pride, etc. As a result of this incorrect belief, it inflicts pain upon itself and is thus the cause of its own misery. Nischay Kshamä (forgiveness) Dharma teaches the Soul to correctly identify itself by encouraging it to contemplate its true nature and hence achieve the state of right belief or Samyak Darshan. It is only by achieving Samyak Darshan that the Soul ceases to inflict pain on itself and attains supreme happiness.

2) Modesty/Humility – UTTAM MARDAV

External View: Wealth, good looks, reputable family or intelligence often lead to pride. Pride means to believe one to be superior to others and to look down on others. By being proud you are measuring your worth by temporary material objects. These objects will either leave you or you will be forced to leave them when you die. These eventualities will cause you unhappiness as a result of the 'dent' caused to your self-worth. Being humble will prevent this.

Internal View: All souls are equal, none being superior or inferior to another. In the words of Srimad Rajchandra: "Sarva Jeev Che Sidh Sum, Je Samje Te Thai – All souls are akin to the Siddha (liberated souls); those who understand this principle will achieve that state." This view encourages you to understand your true nature. All souls have the potential to be liberated souls. The only difference between the liberated souls and those in bondage is that the former have attained liberation as a result of their "effort." With effort, even the latter can achieve liberation.

3) Straightforwardness – UTTAM AARJAV

External View: The action of a deceitful person is to think one thing, speak something else and do something entirely different. There is no harmony in his thought, speech and actions. Such a person loses credibility very quickly and lives in constant anxiety and fear of his deception being exposed. Being straight forward or honest oils the wheel of life. You will be seen to be reliable and trustworthy.

Internal View: Delusion about one's identity is the root cause of unhappiness. Be straightforward to yourself and recognize your true nature. The Soul is made up of countless qualities like knowledge, happiness, effort, faith, and conduct. It has the potential to achieve omniscience (Keval Jnän) and reach a state of supreme bliss. Again, the body, the Karmas, the thoughts and all the emotions are separate from the true nature of the Soul. Only by practicing Nischay Aarjav Dharma will one taste the true happiness that comes from within.

4) Contentment – UTTAM SHAUCH

External View: Be content with the material gains that you have accomplished thus far. Contrary to popular belief, striving for greater material wealth and pleasure will not lead to happiness. Desire for more is a sign that we do not have all that we want. Reducing this desire and being content with what we have leads to satisfaction. Accumulating material objects merely fuels the fire of desire.

Internal View: Contentment or happiness, derived from material objects, is only perceived to be so by a Soul in a state of false belief. The fact is that material objects do not have a quality of happiness and therefore happiness cannot be obtained from them. The perception of "enjoying" material objects is only a temporary perception. This perception rewards the Soul with only misery and nothing else. Real happiness comes from within, as it is the Soul that possesses the quality of happiness.

5) Truth – UTTAM SATYA

External View: If talking is not required, then do not talk. If it is required then only use the minimum number of words, and all must be absolutely true. Talking disturbs the stillness of the mind. Consider the person who lies and lives in fear of being exposed. To support one lie he has to utter a hundred more. He becomes caught up in a tangled web of lies and is seen as untrustworthy and unreliable.

Internal View: Satya comes from the word Sat, which means existence. Existence is a quality of the Soul. Recognizing the Soul's true nature as it really exists and taking shelter in the Soul is practising Nischay Satya Dharma.

6) Self-Restraint – UTTAM SANYAM

External View: Restraining from injury to life. Jains go to great lengths, compared to other world religions, to protect life. This encompasses all living beings, from one-sensed onward. The purpose of not eating root vegetables is that they contain countless one-sensed beings termed "nigod." During Paryushan the Jains also do not eat green vegetables to reduce harm to the lower sensed beings. Also, self-restraint from desires or passions which can lead to pain, and therefore should be avoided.

Internal View:
i) Restraining injury to the self. This has been elaborated upon in Forgiveness (Kshamä) Dharma.

ii) Self restraint from desires or passions. Emotions, e.g. likes, dislikes or anger, lead to misery and need to be eradicated. They are not part of the true nature of the Soul and only arise when the Soul is in a state of false belief. The only method to free oneself from these is to contemplate on the true nature of the Soul and in the process commence the journey to liberation or moksha.

7) Penance – UTTAM TAP

External View: This does not only mean fasting but also includes a reduced diet, restriction of certain types of foods, avoiding tasty foods, etc. The purpose of penance is to keep desires and passions in control. Over-indulgence inevitably leads to misery. Penance leads to an influx of positive Karmas.

Internal View: Meditation prevents the rise of desires and passions in the Soul. In a deep state of meditation the desire to intake food does not arise. The first Tirthankar, Adinath Bhagwan was in such a meditative state for six months, during which he observed Nischay Uttam Tap. Only from the meditative energy from within, he went on for six months with no food.

8) Renunciation – UTTAM TYÄG

External View: Contrary to popular belief, renouncing worldly possessions leads to a life of contentment and assists in keeping desires in check. Renunciation is done at the highest level by monks who renounce not only the household but also their clothes. A person's strength is measured not by the amount of wealth he accumulates but by the amount of wealth he renounces. By this measure the monks and laypeople living balanced, Non-Possessive lives are the richest.

Internal View: Renouncing the emotions, the root cause of misery, is Nischay Uttam Tyag, which is only possible by contemplating on the true nature of the Soul.

9) Non-attachment – UTTAM ÄKINCHANYA

External View: This assists us in detaching from external possessions. Historically, ten possessions are listed in scriptures: land, house, silver, gold, wealth, grain, female servants, male servants, garments and utensils. Of course in today's world, money, investments, car, and clothes are part of our possessions as well. Remaining unattached from these helps control our desires and leads to an influx of punya Karmas.

Internal View: This assists us in being unattached from our internal attachments: false belief, anger, pride, deceit, greed, laughter, liking, disliking, lamentation, fear, disgust, and sexual desire.

10) Supreme Celibacy – UTTAM BRAHMCHARYA

External View: This means not only refraining from sexual intercourse but also includes all pleasures associated with the sense of touch, e.g. desiring for a cool breeze on a hot summer's day or using a cushion for a hard surface. Again this dharma is practiced to keep our desires in check. The monks practice this to the highest degree with all their body, speech and mind. The householder refrains from sexual intercourse with anyone except his or her spouse.

Internal View: Brahmacharya is derived from the words Brahma (Soul) and charya (to dwell). Nischay Brahmacharya means to dwell in your Soul. Only by residing in the Soul you are the master of the Universe. Residing outside your Soul makes you a slave to desires.

Kshamä Väni Parva

This is celebrated two days after the end of the Das Lakshan Parva. With mindful and genuine practice over these 8/10/18 days, our mind, heart, and intellect are strengthened and ready to ask for forgiveness.

On this day we have the courage to meet our friends and relatives (or call them), especially people you have had disagreements, fights, and miscommunication with and ask for forgiveness.

On this day we have the courage to say:

Please forgive me if I have hurt you or have done wrong toward you intentionally or unintentionally (Micchami Dukkadam)

with elders: touch their feet and ask for forgiveness

with youngsters: embrace them and ask for forgiveness

with friends: embrace them and ask for forgiveness

with enemies: meet them or call them and ask for forgiveness

with all living beings and our planet: mentally ask for forgiveness as you may have hurt them in the process of living a Jain Way of Life.

"Conquer anger by forgiveness, pride by humility and deceit by straight-forwardness and greed by contentment." — Mahävir

Source: Shitul Shah (based in London) – Young Jains newsletter, October 2000

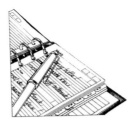

8–10 Days of Living a Jain Way of Life

During Paryushan Parv/Das Lakshan

Paryushan Parv/Das Lakshan are festivals for celebrating the qualities and essence of the Soul. These auspicious 8 or 10 days offer us an opportunity to focus on our spirituality with the hope that we will live a Jain Way of Life for the rest of the year.

Disciplining oneself for these practices is a difficult task. The following activity recommendations are for people of all ages along with point incentives. A family can print this page and give one copy to each member of the family to fill out and add up the points at the end of the festival. A gift can be offered for achieving a certain point target. Each family member should encourage and help others to achieve their best.

Family Member Name: _____ **Date:** _____

(print this and post it in a room where everyone can see it)

Activity	Points per day	Day 1	Day 2	Day 3	Day 4	Day 5	Day 6	Day 7	Day 8	Day 9	Day 10	Total
Recite three Namokar Mantra in the morning and evening with devotion	5											
5 minutes Prayer/Stuti/ meditation after shower	10											
10 minutes of spiritual reading (or go on net and listen to lectures)	10											
Eat at home before dark	5											
Do not eat food with eggs, honey, lard, gelatin	10											

Activity	Points per day	Day 1	Day 2	Day 3	Day 4	Day 5	Day 6	Day 7	Day 8	Day 9	Day 10	Total
Do not eat underground vegetables or food (potato, carrot, etc.)	10											
Go through your clothes and other belongings and donate; donate 0.5% of your earnings	10											
Eat twice in a day Eat once per day Fast (take water)	5 10 20											
Go to temple or gathering to celebrate, listen to discourse	10											
No TV, video/computer games	10											
No feelings of negative passions (anger, deceit, greed, pride)	20											
Total	100+											

Gift Ideas: 100/120 Maximum Possible Points in a Day

Average pts.	Children	Teenagers	Adults
80+/100	Higher value gift card	Non-Violent game for their game machine. Going out for the weekend	Book: massage, relaxation, etc. Meditation classes
50+/100	Gift card to an educational toy store	Celebration at a vegetarian restaurant	Book: kids cooking for their parents

"A person performing penance with a desire of fame or worship does not achieve a genuine penance; so penance should be observed without pomp and show, and one should not flaunt or praise it." — Saman Suttam

Source: Jain Center of Greater Boston Pathshala.

The Practices of Equanimity and Pratikraman

Pratikraman is a practice of confession and repentance and can be done in many different ways. It can be performed at any time but is specifically done on the last day of Paryushan Parv celebration. It includes the following six essentials:

1. Sämäyik (Equanimity)

- The essence of Tirthankar's teachings
- To remain calm and undisturbed
- To discard all sinful activities for a minimum of 48 minutes
- To engage in spiritual activities
- To be free of passions
- To treat all living beings equally
- Perfect Sämäyika is ideal conduct.

Benefits
- Helps calm our mind and temperament
- Enhances equanimity and Soul experience
- Emulating monks/ sädhu's kriya (practices) for a short period of time

2. Chauvisattho – Worshipping Tirthankars

Benefits
- Helps control our passions.
- Purify our beliefs and attain Right Perception.

Praying and appreciating the attributes of the 24 Tirthankars. In Logassa Sutra we offer obeisance to the 24 Tirthankars.

Guru Vandan – Offering Obeisance to Gurus

Respecting and saluting our true spiritual teachers (Ächäryas, Upädhyäys, and Sädhus).

Pratikraman – Turning Back from Transgression

Benefits
- Subdue our ego
- Control our passions
- Develop humility (Vinay)
- Advance spiritually

- "Prati" means "back" and "Kraman" means "to go."
- To go back, review, confess, and repent for bad thoughts and actions in our daily activities.
- Asking forgiveness for our wrongful acts without reservation.
- Vowing to minimize these acts, forgiving others for their faults, and extending friendship.
- To get away from the tendency of finding fault in others,

criticizing others and to develop the habit of self-analysis, self-improvement, and introspection.

- Repentance/atonement.

Kāyotsarg-Meditation

Benefits

- Stop the influx of Karma that obscures the true nature of the Soul.
- Detaches us from the external world.
- Helps us to introspect.

- Becoming detached from the body and tuning with oneself.
- Making the body and mind as steady as possible.
- Concentrating on the feeling that our Soul is separate from our body.

Religious Vows-Pratyākhyna Pachchakhan

Benefits

- Experience the self and not our body.
- Reduce attachment.

- Renouncing certain activities for a predetermined period of time to discipline ourselves.
- Abandonment of things harmful to the Soul.
- Acceptance of things beneficial to the Soul.
- Taking vows, disengaging from worldly objects according to our capabilities.
- Engaging in the process of purification.

MICHHAMI DUKKADAM (I BEG YOUR FORGIVENESS - MAY MY FAULTS BE DISSOLVED)

At the end of the Pratikraman, we become so soft hearted that we are ready to ask for forgiveness.

The following are the items used in Sāmāyik and Pratikraman and their spiritual significance:

Charavalo

- Used for observation of Non-Violence and symbolizes the importance of cleansing our Soul.

Muhapatti (Covering of the mouth)

- Reminder of restraining our speech, to speak only when necessary, and to be humble and courteous.
- Repetition of sutras several times
- Detailed description of code of conduct-activities have changed, motives have not.
- Effective way to purify oneself.
- Religious principles are weaved into daily life. Religion is not just an abstraction.
- Jain prayers are not for obtaining wealth, power, fame or other worldly things.
- Emphasis on humility, introspection, and forgiveness and other divine qualities.

> *First is knowledge, then comes conduct.*
> — Dashavaikalik-sutra, verse 10 Ch. 4

Sources: The Jain Society of Metropolitan Chicago, Jain Pāthashālā Anop Vora – English Pratikraman

Celebrating Thanksgiving – The Jain Way

Between 260 and 300 million turkeys are slaughtered annually in the United States, according to USDA statistics.

Of these, approximately 45 million are killed for Thanksgiving, and 22 million are killed for Christmas. Per capita turkey consumption, which has increased steadily in the United States, averages just below 18 pounds per person. In 1970, turkey consumption per person averaged just 6.4 pounds.

The White House turkey is pardoned and sent to the Washington Zoo each year during Thanksgiving.

Thanksgiving Prayer – The following is a prayer you can do with your family on Thanksgiving. You can also do Namokar Mantra Jap.

Today we give thanks for this vegetarian meal and the people who have labored to harvest and prepare this meal for us. We give thanks for the many lives that have contributed to our lives. We also ask for forgiveness from the living beings that we have harmed, intentionally and unintentionally.

We are grateful for our health and the opportunity to eat with others on this day. We aspire, with compassionate hearts, to use the energy that we gain from this meal and our friends to contribute to the peace and happiness of all living beings.

We pray that all the people of the world will avoid inflicting harm on animals and fellow human beings and practice nonviolence and compassion. We express our sorrow at the suffering of all the turkeys and other animals that are being slaughtered. May peace and compassion grow in ourselves and extend to all around us.

Source: Dr. Jina Shah of Northen California and Jaina Education Committee

Jain Pujäs, Symbols, Temples, History

Jain Philosophy – Mini Overview

Jainism is a religion and a way of live. For thousands of years, Jains have been practicing vegetarianism, yoga, meditation, and environmentalism. Jains believe in the existence of Soul, in each living being, which is eternal and divine. Our purpose in life is to "know ourselves" and that happiness and knowledge exist in me. Jain philosophy has three core practices (essence of Jainism): Non-Violence, Non-Absolutism, and Non-Possessiveness.

Non-Violence (Ahimsa) is compassion and forgiveness in thoughts, words, and deeds toward all living beings. For this reason, Jains are vegetarians.

Non-Absolutism (Anekantvad) or Non-one-sidedness is respect for and seeking others' views. Jains encourage dialogue and harmony with other faiths.

Non-Possessiveness (Aparigrah) is balancing of needs and desires, while staying detached from these possessions. We are all interdependent on each other and we can bring peace to our lives and to those around us. Jains seek spiritual upliftment by practicing Non-Violence, Non-Absolutism, and Non-Possessiveness.

Who Am I? I am a symbiosis of physical and spiritual substances.

Why am I here? I am here to realize who I am and only by managing my passions (Anger, Pride, Ego, Deceit, Greed) can I realize myself.

From where did I come? I come from the past karmic influences.

Where am I going? I am moving toward liberation.

What is the meaning of time? Jainism assumes that the universe, with all its components, is without a beginning or an end, being everlasting and eternal. The wheel of time incessantly revolves like a pendulum. In the first half circle from the descending to the ascending stage where human prosperity, happiness, and life span increases and in the second half circle from the ascending stage to the descending stage where prosperity, happiness, and lifespan decreases.

What is Soul and Karma? Soul is the living-sentient essence. Mahävir explained that from eternity, every living being (Soul) due to its ignorance is in bondage of karmic atoms known as Karma. These Karma are continuously accumulated by our actions of body, mind and speech. Under the influence of Karma, the Soul is habituated to seek pleasures in materialistic belongings and possessions. This is the deep-rooted cause of self-centered violent thoughts, deeds, anger, hatred, greed, and such other vices, which result in further accumulation of Karma. The doctrine of Karma occupies a significant position in the Jain philosophy. It provides a rational and satisfying explanation to the apparently inexplicable phenomena of birth and death, happiness and misery, inequalities in mental and physical attainments, and of the existence of different species of living beings. It explains that the principle governing the successions of life is Karma. Our actions of body, mind, and speech bind us.

How do I achieve liberation from the cycle of life and death? One can get rid of Karma and attain liberation by simultaneously following the path of Right Faith (samyak-darshana), Right Knowledge (samyak-jnän), and Right Conduct (samyak-charitra). The proper knowledge of the six universal substances (six Dravya) and the nine fundamental truths (nine Tattva) is called Right Knowledge and true faith in that knowledge is called Right Faith. The Right Conduct includes Non-Violence, self-purification, compassion, penance, austerity, and meditation.

Jainism strives for the realization of the highest perfection of man, which in its original purity is free from all pain, suffering, and the bondage of birth and death.

Karma Classification

The Six Universal Substances are:

Soul or Consciousness – Jiv – Living substance
Matter – Pudgal – Non-living substance
Medium of motion – Dharma – Non-living substance
Medium of rest – Adharma – Non-living substance
Space – Akas – Non-living substance
Time – Käl or Samay – Non-living substance

Ghati Karmas (removal of these are needed to attain Omniscience – Keval Jnän): View/Faith deluding, Obstructing, Perception/Intuition Covering, Knowledge Covering.

Aghati Karmas (removal of these are needed to attain Liberation): lifespan, body, status, feeling producing.

The Nine Tattvas (Fundamentals) are:

Jiv – Soul or living being (Consciousness)
Ajiv – Non-living substances
Äsrav – Cause of the influx of Karma
Bandha – Bondage of Karma
Punya – Meritorious Karma
Pap – Sin or demeritorious Karma
Samvara – Stoppage or arrest of the influx of Karma
Nirjarä – Shedding of the accumulated Karma
Moksha – Total liberation from Karma

Doors of Inflow of Karmas

The first and foremost door to the inflow of Karmas is Mithyätva. This is irrational perception of reality or nature (rational perception is understanding and belief in Soul, Karma, and their relationship and dynamics). The other doors of inflow of Karmas include:

4 types of passions (Anger, Pride-Ego, Deceit, Greed)
5 types of senses (Touch, Taste, Smell, Sight, Hearing)
5 types indulgences (Causing Injury, Lying, Stealing, Incontinence, Possessiveness).

Ethical Code

The supreme ideal of the Jain religion is Non-Violence (Ahimsa), equal kindness, and reverence for all forms of life in speech, thought, and action. Above all, it is a religion of love and compassion to all living beings. At the heart of Right Conduct for Jains lie the five great vows.

These vows cannot be fully implemented without the acceptance of a philosophy of Non-Absolutism (Anekantvad) and the theory of relativity (Syadvad). Monks and nuns follow these vows strictly and totally, while the common people follow the vows as far as their lifestyles will permit.

> *Non-Violence (Ahimsa)* – Not to cause harm to any living beings
> *Truthfulness (Satya)* – To speak the harmless truth only
> *Non-stealing (Asteya)* – Not to take anything not properly given
> *Chastity (Brahmacharya)* – Not to indulge in sensual pleasure
> *Non-Possession/Non-Attachment (Aparigraha)* – Complete detachment from people, places, and material things

Twelve Vows of Layman

Five Main Vows of Limited Nature (Anuvratas): 1) Ahimsa; 2) Satya; 3) Achaurya (Non-Stealing); 4) Bhramcharaya (Chastity); 5) Aparigraha (Non-Attachment).

Three Merit Vows (Gun-vrats) 1) Dik Vrat (Limited area of activity vow); 2) Bhog-Upbhog Vrat (Limited use of consumable and non-consumable items vow); 3) Anartha-dand Vrat (Avoidance of purposeless sins vow).

Four Disciplinary Vows (Siksha-vratas) limited duration 1) Sämäyik, Meditation; 2) Activity; 3) Ascetic's life; 4) Limited charity.

Ten Virtues (Das Lakshan Dharma)

1) Uttam Kshamä, supreme forbearance; *2) Uttam Märdav*, supreme gentleness; *3) Uttam Arjav*, supreme uprightness; *4) Uttam Shauch*, supreme purity; *5) Uttam Satya*, supreme truth; *6) Uttam Sanyam*, supreme restraint; *7) Uttam Tap*, supreme austerity; *8) Uttam Tyäga*, supreme renunciation; *9) Uttam Äkinchanya*, supreme lack of possession; *10) Uttam Brahmcharya*, supreme chastity.

Six Avshashaks (Essentials)

1) Samayik, a state of total equanimity; *2) Chauvisantho*, prayers to the 24 Jinas; *3) Vandana*, offering salutations to sädhus (monks) and sädhvis (nuns); *4) Pratikraman*, realizing what we have done wrong and annotating on it; *5) Kayotsarga*, meditation of the Soul; *6) Prätyakhyän*, renunciation.

14 Gunsthanas

These are the 14 stages a person must pass through to achieve liberation. ***Lowest stage: 1)*** *Mithyätva Gunasthänak*, stage of false beliefs with intense raag and dwesh; 2) *Sasvädan,* the stage of having tasted the righteousness; 3) *Samyak-Mithyädrashti,* stage of fluctuation between the false and right belief; 4) *Avirati-samyakdrashti,* the stage of the right belief but no renunciation; 5) *Deshvirati,* the stage of the right belief with the partial renunciation; 6) *Sarvavirti or Pramatt samyati,* the stage of the total renunciation; 7) *Apramatt samyati,* the stage of the total renunciation and no carelessness; 8) *Nivritti-Bädar,* the stage of an extraordinary efforts; 9) *Anivritti-Bädar,* the stage of almost passionless state; 10) *Sukshma samparay,* the stage of the subtle greed; 11) *Upashant Kashay,* the stage of the passionless state by the suppression; 12) *Kshina Kashay,* the passionless stage; 13) *Sayogi kevali,* the stage of the omniscient with activities; ***Highest:*** *14) Ayogi kevali,* the stage of the omniscient without activities. The fourteenth Gunasthän is for a moment of time as the Soul attains Nirvana and moves to Siddhashilä (see Jain Universe symbol).

12 Bhävanäs (12 Reflections)

1) Anitya, Impermanence of the world, alone; 2) *Asharan*– Birth is inevitably followed by death, helpless in the face of death; 3) *Samsär*, Worldly life is an ocean of illusion. No permanent relationship; 4) *Ekatva*, Aloneness. There is absolute solitude of each Soul; 5) *Anyatva*, Separateness – Try to know the inner-self to attain "Pure-Self." 6) *Ashuchi*, Impureness of the body; 7) *Äsrav*, Inflow of Karmic Fusion; 8) *Samvar*, Karmic shield is antidote to Äsrav, stops influx of Karma; 9) *Nirjarä*, to discard – to separate – liberate, Shedding of Karma from Soul; 10) *Lokasvarup*, To reflect about the Universe; 11) *Bodhi Durlabh*, Unattainability of Right Perception, Right Knowledge, and Right Conduct; 12) *Dharma,* Teachings of the Thirthankar -Arihant.

Parasparopagraho Jivänäm

Souls influence each other through service which may be favorable or unfavorable.

They cannot live independently of one another.

They must bear the karmic results individually.

They create a common environment and live together in wealth and woe.

Five Samitis (Conduct)

1) Iryä Samiti: regulation of walking. **2) Bhäshä Samiti:** regulation of speaking. Avoid the eight faults of speech during conversation (anger, pride, deceit, greed, laughter, fear, gossip, and slander). Always use sinless and concise speech. **3) Eshanä Samiti**: regulation of begging. Monks should search and obtain pure foods. **4) Ädäna Nikshepanä Samiti:** regulation of taking or keeping. One should lay down or take up an article of use very carefully so as not to endanger the life of small creatures and insects. **5) Utsarga Samiti:** regulation of disposal of waste properly.

Three Guptis

1) Man Gupti: regulation of mind. One should guard one's mind from impure thoughts such as anger, hatred, cursing, greed, jealousy, ego, etc. Always be forgiving and devote the mind to pious meditation.

2) Vachan Gupti: regulation of speech. One should guard his speech so that it might not utter harmful, harsh, careless, foul, senseless, embarrassing, or bad language.

3) Kay Gupti: regulation of bodily activity. One should guard movement of his body, so as not to hurt others, walking with an eye on the path so as not to harm or kill an innocent life such as ants, bugs, etc. One should not daydream while doing any activity. Develop decent behavior and manners.

"Dynamic media (motion), Static media (inertia), Space, Matter, Souls, and Time are the substances of the Universe."
— Tattvarth Sutra by Umäsväti

Source: Pravin Shah, JAINA Education Committee

Jain Pujäs

Pujä is a ritual and another form of meditation. Its purpose is to break the barriers of the worldly attachments and desires, and liberate the Soul. There are two types of pujä:

– Dravya Pujä (offering of material)

– Bhav Pujä (deep feeling and meditation).

Dravya pujä should be done together with Bhav pujä. During the pujä, material offerings are made. These are merely symbolic and are for the benefit of the offerer. The action and ritual of offering keeps the mind in Bhav mode (meditative). The lively atmosphere of a group Pujä enhances focus and meditation. The symbolism of a puja is strong and focuses on virtues of Arihantas and Tirthankars, and giving up all attachment. Above all, puja is not performed with a desire for any material goal. There are some traditions within Jainism which have no pujäs at all and are focused on meditation though scripture reading and philosophical discussions.

Jain Pujä (Ashta Prakäri Pujä and Dev Shästra Guru Pujä)

There are different types of pujä being performed for various religious and social ceremonies. The following are the types of items used for puja. The meaning of material offerings are slightly different based on the type of puja. Described below are the meanings for Ashta Prakäri (Eight offerings) and Dev Shästra Guru Pujä (Arihant/God, Scriptures, and Guru).

Preparation for Pujä:

Body Cleansing: A bath should be taken before the pujä. During bathing and until one reaches the temple, the mind should be in a spiritual mode. One should not carry any leather article such as belts, purses, leather cell phone covers, etc.

Traveling to the temple: Devotional and spiritual music and prayers can be played in the car. While walking from the parking lot to the temple, care should be observed that no living beings are harmed due to one's carelessness.

Clothes: Clean, washed clothes. In some traditions only dhoti or Kurta Pajama is preferred.

Abhishek: The idol Abhishek (pouring of water over the idol) may take place before the pujä. This is a symbolism of washing one's dirt or bad Karmas. While doing Abhishek, visualize that ones own desires and worldly attachment are washing away.

Reciting of prayers: While getting ready for pujä, prayers should be recited with utmost concentration.

Body purification: Place kesar (saffron paste) on ring finger and anoint the forehead, left and right earlobe, neck, and near the belly button to symbolize cleanliness of the body.

Ashta Prakāri Pujā

1. Jala Pujā: (Water)

My Soul, a kalash made of knowledge,
I fill, with the water of equanimity.
And as I bathe the Arihant,
My Karmas are washed away.

Water symbolizes the ocean. Every living being continuously travels through the cycles of birth, life, death, and misery. This pujā reminds me that I should live my life with honesty, truthfulness, love and compassion toward all living beings. This way one will be able to end the cycle of life and death by attaining total knowledge and Moksha or liberation. The path of liberation is Samyak Darshan (Right Perception), Samyak Jnān (Right Knowledge) and Samyak Charitra (Right Conduct).

Due to my wrong faith, I have indulged in the pleasures of the senses and was attracted to the materialistic human body. Now I have come to offer you the pure water to wash off my wrong faith and as a result to destroy my cycles of life and death.

2. Chandan Pujā: (Sandal-wood)

He whose face beams with tranquility within
The one whose very nature is tranquil
To that Arihant I worship
My Soul, to make tranquil.

Chandan symbolizes Knowledge (Jnān). During this pujā one should reflect on Right Knowledge. Right Knowledge means proper understanding of reality which includes Soul, Karma, and their relationship. Jainism believes that the Path of Knowledge is the main path to attain liberation. Bhakti or Devotion helps in the early stages of one's effort for liberation.

3. Pushpa Pujā: (Flower)

Perfumed, a flower in full bloom I hold;
For this pujā, which destroys the misery of birth.
Just as a bee hovers around the flower;
To be around you always,
I ask that samkit (Right Perception) be imprinted upon me.

Flower symbolizes conduct. My conduct should be like a flower, which provides fragrance and beauty to all living beings without discrimination. I should live my life like a flower full of love and compassion toward all living beings.

4. Dhup Pujā: (Incense)

Meditation illuminates the dense darkness,
Just as I offer the incense before the beautiful eyes of the Jina
Driving away the bad smell of wrong faith, The innate nature of the Soul emerges.

Dhup symbolizes ascetic life. While burning itself, Dhup provides fragrance to others. Similarly true monks and nuns spend their entire life selflessly for the benefit of all living beings. This pujā reminds me that I should thrive for an ascetic life which ultimately leads to liberation.

5. Deepak Pujā: (Candle)

Like a lamp, help us distinguish between good and bad
To avoid sorrow in this world
And one day, my internal lamp of knowledge will
Illuminate the entire universe.

The flame of Deepak represents pure consciousness or a Soul without any bondage or a Liberated Soul. Such a Soul is called Siddha or God. The ultimate goal of every living being is to live a life free of passions and become liberated from Karma. By doing this pujā I remind myself to follow Five Great Vows: Non-Violence, Truthfulness, Non-stealing, Chastity and Non-possession. Ultimately these proper conducts coupled with Right Perception and Right Knowledge will lead to liberation.

6. Akshat Pujã: (Rice)

Pure unbroken akshat I hold
And draw this large Nandyãvart
In the presence of my lord,
I wish all my worldliness
Will postpone indefinitely.

The rice is non-fertile One cannot grow rice plants by seeding the household rice. Symbolically it means that rice is the last birth. By doing this pujã one should thrive to put all the efforts in the life in such a way that this life becomes one's last life and after the end of this life one will be liberated and will not be reborn again.

7. Naivedya Pujã: (Tasty Food)

Many a times I have gone hungry
And traveled through many lives
O Pure One! Without a trace of desire,
Do satiate me eternally.

Naivedya symbolizes a tasty food. By doing this pujã, one should thrive to reduce or eliminate the attachment to tasty food. Healthy food is essential for survival, however one should not live for eating tasty foods. The ultimate aim in one's life is to attain a life where no food is essential for our existence and that is the life of a liberated Soul, who lives in Moksha forever in ultimate bliss.

8. Fal Pujã: (Fruit)

Just as Indra and other devs
Out of their extreme love for you,
I bring along 'fruits' to worship.
Upon meeting you, O Supreme Soul,
I renounce worldly aspirations
And desire only Moksha
As the fruit of all my actions.

Fruit symbolizes Moksha or Liberation. If we live our life without any attachment to worldly affairs, continue to perform our duty without any expectation and reward, be witness to all the incidents that occurred surrounding and within us, truly follow ascetic life, and have a love and compassion to all living beings, we will attain the fruit of Moksha or liberation. This is the last Pujã symbolizing the ultimate achievement of our life.

Dev Shãstra Guru Pujã

This pujã worships the Dev, Shãstra, and Guru.

- Dev means God or Arihant or Siddha.

- Shãstra means Scriptures.

- Guru means Teachers or one who possesses "real knowledge."

By worshipping Dev, Shãstra, and Guru, we draw attention to these three entities as a means for our path to liberation.

Invocation

Invocation begins with Namokar Mantra and Chattari mangalam, then say "om jay jay jay, namostu, namostu, namostu" and chant Namokar Mantra.

The rays of sun of Siddhas illuminate; I bow to Siddhas, scriptures, and monks who are on the path of Right Perception, Knowledge, and Conduct. I ask Siddha, scriptures, and monks to settle in my mind while I do this pujã. Here we invite Dev, Shãstra, and Guru to the pujã so we can pray to them. This is done by taking three full cloves and holding one clove at a time between the two ring fingers, while keeping the clove head pointed forward while chanting the sthapana, offer the cloves.

First clove: think of Dev, Shästra, and Guru to come into our thoughts.

Second clove: think of Dev, Shästra, and Guru to stay into our thoughts.

Third clove: think of Dev, Shästra, and Guru to be near me.

Offerings

The offerings here are similar to the previous pujä except that flowers, food, candle, and fruits are symbolically replaced by safforn covered rice, white coconut, saffron covered coconut, and almond. The eight offerings are: Jal (water), Chandan (sandalwood), Askhat (rice), Pushpa (yellow rice), Navivedya (white coconut), Deep (yellow coconut), Dhoop (incense), Fal (almond in its shell), and Argh (mixture of all eight offerings). The significance of these offerings are the same as in the Ashta Prakäri pujä.

Jaimala and Shanti Päth

Barah Bhävanä (12 Reflections) is sung. After that, Shanti Päth, prayer of peace for all living beings, is said and then Namokar mantra is chanted 9 times.

Closing – Forgiveness

At the conclusion, Visarjan (closing) prayer is said, which means knowingly or unknowingly if I have committed any mistakes during the Pujä, please forgive me.

"Mahävir proclaimed in India that religion is a reality and not a mere social convention. It is really true that salvation cannot be had by merely observing external ceremonies. Religion cannot make any difference between man and man." — Dr. Rabindranath Tagore

---

http://www.jaina.org/educationcommittee/
education_material/C15_Jain_Rituals_and_Holidays/
www.jainpujä.com – Excellent site for online streaming pujä with temple graphics
Preeti Jain, Jain Center of Greater Boston

Jain Symbols

Jain Universe

Jain traditions have several symbols. The outline of this symbol is Jain Universe (Lok). The lower part of the symbol represents the seven hells (Naraki). The middle part of the universe contains the Earth and the planets (Manushyalok). The upper part contains the heavenly abodes (Devlok) of all the celestial beings and abode of the Siddhas (Siddhashila). Jains

LIVE AND LET LIVE

believe that this universe was neither created by anyone, nor can it be destroyed by anyone. It may change its form, but otherwise, it has always been and will always be here.

Digit of the Moon represents the region beyond the three worlds wherein reside the liberated souls (Siddhas). It is known as the Siddhashila. In order to achieve this stage, a Soul must destroy all attached Karmas.

Three Dots represent the Jain path of liberation (Jain trinity): Right Perception (Samyak Darshan), Right Knowledge (Samyak Jnän), and Right Conduct (Samyak Charitra), which together lead to liberation. The Right Knowledge means having the knowledge that Soul and body are separate and that the Soul, not the body, attains the salvation. The Right Perception means

one must have faith in the guidance of Jinas, who were omniscient. The Right Conduct means that our actions should be grounded in Non-Violence, Non-Absolutism, and Non-Possessiveness.

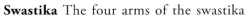

Swastika The four arms of the swastika remind us that during the cycles of birth and death we may be born into any one of the four destinies: heavenly beings, human beings, animal beings, (including birds, bugs, and plants) and hellish beings. Our aim should be the liberation and not the rebirth. To show how we can do this, the swastika reminds us that we should become the pillars of the fourfold Jain Sangh. The four pillars of the Jain Sangh are sädhus (monks), sädhvis (nuns), shrävaks (layman), and shrävikas (laywomen). This means that first, we should strive to be a true shrävaks or shrävikas, and when we are ready to overcome our social attachments, we should renounce the worldly life and follow the path of a sädhu or sädhvi to be liberated. The Swastika symbol was taken by Hitler from this symbol and but was turned counter clockwise.

Palm of the Hand signifies this assurance; "do not be afraid," indicating that human beings, which are suffering due to karmic bondage; do not need to be disheartened. The raised hand also means stop. The word in the center of the wheel is "Ahimsa."

Ahimsa means non-violence. Between these two, they remind us to stop for a minute and be mindful of our actions, thoughts, and speech. This gives us a chance to scrutinize our activities to be sure that they will not hurt anyone by our words, thoughts, or actions. We must not ask or encourage others to take part in any harmful activity. The wheel in the hand shows that if we are not careful and ignore these warnings and carry on violent activities, then just as the wheel goes round and round, we will go round and round through the cycles of violence and birth and death.

Wheel of Dharma (Chakra) with 24 spokes represents the religion preached by the 24 Jain Tirthankars consisting of non-violence (Ahimsa) and other virtues.

The outline figure represents the Jain description of the shape of the universe, resembling a person standing with feet apart and arms resting on both hips.

Arhum – mantra represents all vowels and consonant sounds used in Sanskrit alphabet. While mediating on this mantra, one focuses on the silent sound of the universe.

Significance of OM

The word OM, an acronym of five supreme spiritual guides, made of five letters (a, a, a, u and m) of Arhat (Enlightened Teachers), Ashariri (Siddha – the Liberated Souls), Āchārya (Heads of Religious Order), Upādhyāya (Teachers) and Muni (Monks and Nuns).[15] In addition to this, OM has other meanings also:

- OM means completeness. It is a symbolic word meaning infinite, the perfect, and the eternal. Upon attaining omniscience, the body of the Arihantas emanates Om.

- The great yogis focus on this letter in their meditation day after day.

- OM sounds like Aum which is the seat of the five benedictions (salutations of the supreme being)

- OM represents Divyadhvani (the voice of Arihanta, Enlightened Teacher).

- OM represents pranav mantra used as the point focus in meditation by great yogis.

- OM links to destruction of knowledge obscuring Karma (Gyanavaran Karma).[16]

- OM represents the sum total of five special names given to Tirthankar (Enlightened Teacher) at the times of five Kalyans, respectively Satyojata, Vamadev, Aghora, Isana and Purusha.

- OM represents Brahma which is the Paramatma in the Hindu tradition.

> Omkaram bindu samyuktam, nityam dhyayantu yoginaha;
> Kamadam mokshadam chaiv, Omkaraya namo namaha

- www.JainWorld.com, www.jaina.org/artexhibit by Sudhir Shah, www.jainpushp.org/symbols.htm
- Prof. C. Devakumar (cdevkumar@yahoo.com)
[15] In Saman Suttam (Sutra No,.12)
[16] Dhavala Āgam II from South Indian palm leaf writings.

Jain History

Jainism is the oldest religion Almost all the scholars agree that Jainism has pre-Aryan roots in the cultural history of India. As Dr. A.N. Upadhye remarked, "The origins of Jainism go back to the prehistoric times. They are to be sought in the fertile valley of Ganga, where they flourished in the past, even before the advent of Aryans with their priestly religion, a society of recluses who laid much stress on individual exertion, on practice of a code of morality and devotion to austerities, as means of attaining religious Summum Bonum."[17]

"There is truth in the Jain idea that their religion goes back to a remote antiquity, the antiquity in question being that of the pre-Aryan, so called Dravidian illuminated by the discovery of a series of great late stone-age cities in Indus valley, dating back to third and perhaps even fourth millennium B.C."[18]

Buddha had practiced Jainism In the Buddhist scripture Majjima Nikaya, Buddha himself tells us about his ascetic life and its ordinances, which are in conformity with the Jain monk's code of conduct. He says, "Thus far, SariPutta, did I go in my penance? I went without clothes. I licked my food from my hands. I took no food that was brought or meant especially for me. I accepted no invitation to a meal." Mrs. Rhys Davis has observed that Buddha found his two teachers Alara and Uddaka at Vaisali and started his religious life as a Jain.[19]

Established before Hinduism Some historians think that Jainism existed, no doubt, prior to Buddhism, but it is a protestant creed which revolted against the sacrifices of the Vedic cult. The advanced researchers show that the above stand has no foundation. The respectable and reliable sacred books of the Hindus themselves establish the most ancient nature of Jain thought. Rigveda, the oldest Hindu scripture refers to Lord Rishabhdev, who was the founder of Jainism. It also talks about Vaman Avtar incarnation, who is the 15th incarnation amongst the 24 incarnations of Jains. Rishabh's name comes as the ninth incarnation Vishnu. Rishabh's name occurs before Vaman or Dwarf Ram, Krishna, and Buddha incarnations. Therefore it is quite clear that Rishabh must have flourished long before the composition of Rigveda. The great scholar Dr. S. Radhakrishnan, ex-president of Indian Union, in his 'India Philosophy' had observed, "Jain tradition ascribes the origin of the system to Rishabhadev, the first Tirthankar. There is no doubt that Jainism prevailed even before Mahävir or Parsvanath. The Yajurveda mentions the name of three Tirthankars-Rishabh, Ajitnath and Arishtanemi. The Bhagwat Puran endorses the view that Rishabhadev was the founder of Jainism." (Vol. II, p. 286).[20]

Jain Historical Time Line

	Jain Event	Indian Event	World Event
Infinite time to 8th Century BC	Time of the first 22 Jain Tirthankars (Jain religion propagators who have attained enlightenment) Adinath to Neminath	Vedic Times	Moses
8th to 3rd Century BC	Time of Parsvanath (23rd) and Mahãvir Swami (24th)	Mahabharata Ramayana	Pythagorus, Confucius
3rd Century BC to 5th Century AD	Jainism evolves into several different sects, the main two sects being Shvetãmbara (those who are white clad) and Digambar (sky clad). Despite some difference in practices between these two groups, both still maintain the same fundamentals and principles of Jainism	King Asoka, great ruler of India Decimal System invented in India	Jesus Buddhism spreads in Asia
5th to 13th Century AD	Several distinguished Ãchãryas emerge in India and many modern Jain communities emerge within India Jainism gains great support from Indian Kings Jains contribute to Indian Literature	Muslim and Turkish invasions in India Buddhism declines in India	Muhammad Islam spreads
13th to 1526 AD	Jain communities evolve	Sikhism emerges	
1526 to 1818 AD	Several Jain sects emerge	Mughals rule India	
1818 AD to Present Time	Shrimad Rajchandra (Mahatma Gandhi's spiritual guru) and Pujya Kanjiswami evolved as reformers. Virchand Raghavji represented Jainism at the first World Religion Conference in Chicago in 1893; Jainism spreads worldwide (U.S., UK, Europe, Japan) Sushil Kumarji and Chitrabhanuji preach Jainism in America First Jain organizations in New York and Boston and first temple in Boston.	Swami Vivekananda Tagore prominent in India; Mahatma Gandhi leads India to independence	Buddhism and the ISKCON spread to the Western World, World Wars I & II

Archeological Evidence

The excavations made at Mohenjodaro and Harappa show that Jainism existed five thousands years ago. The pose of the standing deities on the Indus seals resembles the standing image of Rishabhdev obtained from Mathura.

The poet Jinasena in his Mahapurana has spoken of Rishabha as Yogishwara.

Indus valley excavated material glaringly establishes the fact that the founder of Jainism belonged to the pre-Vedic period. The nude Jain idol of 320 B.C. in Patna Museum, of Lohanipur helps us to support the above contention.[19]

Encounter with Alexander

A glance over the glorious past of Jainism reveals the fact that the lives of Rishabhdev and the succeeding 23 Tirthankars had deeply impressed the entire world culture. When Alexander invaded India he came across a host of nude Jain saints in Taxila, whom the Greek writers call 'Gymnosophists.' The Greek word connotes the nude philosopher. The mystic group of Israel, called the Essenes, was much influenced by these 'Gymnosophists,' who were preaching their message of Ahimsa, to the people of Alexandria in Egypt. Historical records tell us that the Greeks were much influenced by Jain thoughts. Alexander had taken one Jain saint, Calanes, with him to his country.[21]

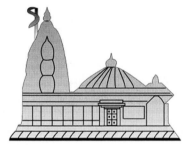

"That which is old become so by passage of time. That which is new is also going to become old. Old does not mean stable or irrefutable. Who would accept without examination, what has been labeled as old?"
— Dwatrinshika of Siddhasen Diwarkar

Source: The University of Michigan – Study Guide http://www.jainworld.com/education/seniors/senles22.htm

[17] See: *A Cultural History of India*, Clarendon Press, Oxford, P. 100

[18] Prof. Zimmer: *Myths and symbols in India Art and Civilization and Philosophies of India*, Ed. Joseph Campbell, see editorial, p. 60

[19] Diwakar S. C., *Glimpse of Jainism*, Published by Shri Bharatvarshiya Digambar Jain Mahasabha

[20] Prof. Buhler: "Indian Sect of Jainism"

[21] Mehta T. U., *The Path of Arhat A Religious Democracy*, Published by Parsvanath Sodhapitha

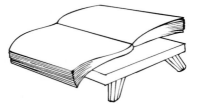

Jain Scriptures

Jain scriptures are a cross between many different disciplines: philosophy, psychology, sociology, biology, chemistry, astronomy, and logic. There are thousands of Jain scriptures and many are believed to have been lost by constant invasion and desecration of Jain temples by outside conquerors. Some of these scriptures were compiled by Ganadhars (Mahävir's direct disciple) and Shruta-Kevalis (scholars of scriptures in lineage of Gandadhars), and are known as Ägam literature. These texts are the Holy Scriptures of the Jain religion. The Jain Ägams consisted of 1) 14 Purvas, 2) 12 Anga-Pravishtha-Ägams and 3) Anga-Bahya-Ägams (34 for Shvetämbar Murtipujäk, 21 for Shvetämbar Sthanakavasi and 14 for Digambar).

All Jain sects agree that 14 Purvas, Drashtivada, and the 12th Anga-Pravishtha-Ägam are extinct. Digambars believe that all Jain Ägams are extinct, where as Shvetämbars accept the existing Jain Ägams as authentic teachings of Lord Mahävir. However, Shvetämbar Murtipujäk believe there are 34 Anga-Bahya-Ägams while Shvetämbar Sthanakavasi believe that there are 21 Anga-Bahya-Ägams.

Some Sacred Books

All Jain sects consider Tattvärtha Sutra unanimously as the main Jain scriptures today. The others include Uttaradhyayan Sutra (Shvetämbar scripture) and Samaysar (Digambar sacred book). These are the three main Jain sacred books today.

Tattvärtha-Sutra

Written in Sanskrit language by Umäsväti (also known as Umänswämi) around 200-400 AD. It focuses on the process we apply even today to acquire knowledge. The first verse of the first chapter is "Samyag Darshan Jnän Charitrani Moksha Märgah," which means Right Perception, Right Knowledge, and Right Conduct collectively are the only path to liberation (Moksha). The fourth verse mentions the seven elements. The rest of the first chapter deals with the process of cognition and details different types of knowledge. The details about Right Conduct are included in chapters eight and nine.

The second, third and fourth chapters deal with the Soul (Jiv). The fifth chapter describes the Non-Soul (Ajiv). The sixth, seventh and eighth chapters describe the various types of Karmas and their manifestations, and the inflow and the bondage of Karmas (Bandh and Äsrav). Chapter nine describes the stoppage and shedding of Karmas (Samvar and Nirjarä). Chapter ten is about the complete liberation Moksha (Moksha) of the Soul.

Uttarädhyayan Sutra

Uttaradhyayan Sutra contains the last sermons of Lord Mahävir available with the translations in many languages. The text describes four insights: human life, sermons of the Jins, Right or rational vision, and Right Conduct of restraints.

Samaysär

Ächärya Shri Kundkund Swami wrote Samaysär around 100 AD. This book has 415 aphorisms and it is divided into nine chapters.

Modern Jain Texts

There are hundreds of excellent modern Jain texts available. One was written by a Jain and Buddhist professor from the University of California at Berkeley, Dr. Padmanath Jaini, called the *Jain Path of Purification*. Another one, which is very easy to read and ideal for a college text book on Jainism, is *Jainism and the New Spirituality* by Dr. Vastupal Parikh. JAINA Education Committee under the leadership of Pravin Shah has developed some of most extensive Jain English publications.

Important Jain Scriptures

Name of Scripture	Author	Description
Acharänga Sutra (Ayarang)	Mahävir Swami; passed on by word-of-mouth until eventually written down by various monks and scholars	One of several Ägams; this one describes the conduct and behavior of ascetic life and the description of the penance of Lord Mahävir. This is the oldest Ägam from a linguistic point of view.
Kalpa Sutra	Bhadrabahu	Describes the lives of Jinas. Narrates the life of Mahävir. Lists the rules for Yatis.
Pravachansär	Ächärya Kundkund	In this sutra, all the Tirthankars and Arihants are praised for their achievements of pure faith, knowledge, and perfect conduct.
Tattvärth-Sutra	Ächärya Umäsväti (200-400 AD)	The first Jain text in sutra form; deals with the process of cognition and details about different types of knowledge; provides further insight about the Soul; discusses Non-Soul (Ajiva); discusses the influx and bondage of Karma; explains the liberation of the Soul (Moksha).
Anekantajayapatäkä	Haribhadra Suri (c.700-c.770)	This scripture discusses *The Victory Banner of Relativism* and his other works teach tolerance for other traditions.

Name of Scripture	Author	Description
Prashamarati Prakaran	Umäsväti Vachak	Divided into chapters, with each chapter providing detailed explanations of the many aspects of Jainism, including the 4 passions, 8 kinds of Karma, cycle of birth/death, eight kinds of prides, code of conduct, 12 Bhävanäs, six substances, etc.
Chhah Dhala	Pandit Daulat Ram	Metrical composition of six verses; contains a condensed version of Jain philosophy.
Purushartha-Siddhupäy	Ächärya Amrit Chandra Suri	Defines the meaning of Vyavähar and Nishchaya, the real and unreal; also the nature and role of Karma to the Jiva.
Saman Suttam	Kshullak Jinendra Varni	This text is grouped into four parts: Source of Illumination, Path of liberation, Metaphysics, and Relativity.
Niyamsär	Kundkund Ächärya	Broken down into 12 categories: jiva, ajiva, pure thought activity, practical Right Conduct, repentance, renunciation, confession, expiation, supreme equanimity, supreme devotion, real independence, pure consciousness.
Ashta Pahuda	Kundkund	Outlines the right path in terms of faith, scripture, conduct, enlightenment, realization, emancipation, insignia, and virtue.
Dravya Samgraha	Nemi Chandra Siddhanta Chakravarti	Distinguishes the differences between Jiva and Ajiva.
Samaysär	Kundkund Ächärya	Expresses the causes of Karma and the ways in which one can realize and overcome them; explains the difference between jiva/ajiva and Karma theory.
Ancillary Shästra		A class of important scriptures which acts as manual for divine worship; explains the proper procedure for external worship of idols, etc.; provides great details about ontology and cosmology, liberation, devotion, meditation, philosophy of mantras, mystic diagrams, charms and spells, temple-building, image-making, domestic observances, social rules, public festivals, etc.

Anga-pravishtä Ägams:

1. Acharanga Sutra (Ayaranga): One of several Ägams; describes the conduct and behavior of ascetic life and the description of the penance of Lord Mahävir. This is the oldest Ägam from a linguistic point of view.

2. Sutra-krtäng Sutra (Suyagadanga-sutta): Describes Non-Violence, Jain metaphysics, and the refutation of other religious theories such as Kriya Vada, Akriya-vada, Ajnanvada, and Vinaya-vada.

3. Sthänang Sutra (Thananga-sutta): Defines and catalogs the main substances of the Jain metaphysics.

4. Samavayang Sutra: This Ägam defines and cataloges the main substances of the Jain religion from a different perspective than the Sthananga Sutra.

5. Vyakhyä Prajnapti or Bhagavati Sutra (Viyah Pannati): Explains the subtle knowledge of Soul, matter, and other related subjects. Thirty-six thousands (36,000) questions and answers are presented in discussion form. It is the largest of the eleven Anga-Pravishta-Ägams.

6. Jnätä Dharma Kathanga Sutra (Naya-dhamma-kaha-sutta): Explains Jain principles through examples and stories. This text is very useful in understanding the mode of Lord Mahävir's religious preaching.

7. Upasäka Dashänga Sutra (Uvasagadasäo): Explains the code of conduct of the ten lay followers (Shrävaks) of Lord Mahävir. This Ägam is very useful for understanding the code and conduct of lay followers (Shrävak Dharma).

8. Antakrit-dashanga Sutra (Antagadadasao): Tells the stories of ten sacred monks attaining liberation (Moksha) by destroying their Karmas.

9. Anuttarop-pätika Dashanga Sutra (Anuttarovavaiya Dasao): Has the stories of 10 additional sacred monks who attained the top-most heaven, known as Anuttara heaven.

10. Prashna Vyäkaran Sutra (Panha Vagaranam): Describes the five great vows (Maha-vratas) and the five worst sins defined in the Jain religion.

11. Vipak Sutra (Vivaga-suyam): Explains the results of good and bad Karmas through several stories.

12. Drashtivada Sutra: The twelfth Anga-Pravishtha-Ägams Drashtivada is considered lost by all Jain Sects. The description, which is found in the other Jain Sutras relating to Drashtivada, indicates that this Anga-Pravishtha-Ägam was the largest of all Ägam Sutras. It was classified in five parts, (1) Parikarma (2) Sutra (3) Purvagat (4) Pratham-Anuyog and (5) Chulika. The third part, Purvagata contained 14 Purvas. They contained the Jain religion's endless treasure of knowledge on every subject.

"In conclusion, let me assert my conviction that Jainism is an original system, quite distinct and independent from all others; and that therefore it is of great importance for the study of philosophical thoughts and religious life in ancient India."
— Dr. Herman Jacobi

Source: Pravin Shah – Jain Education Committee
Ancient Scriptures Come Alive, a multi-media presentation on Tattvärth-Sutra, by Jain Center to Greater Boston, Level 6 Pathshala at JAINA Convention, Toronto 1997

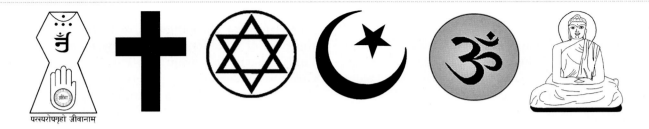

परस्परोपग्रहो जीवानाम्

Jainism and Other Religions

Jainism shares commonality with other religions but is also unique in its focus and practice of Ahimsa (Non-Violence). Even just the definition of God is so different in different traditions: Hindus acknowledge multitudes of gods and goddesses; Buddhists say there is no deity; New Age followers believe they are God; Muslims believe in a powerful but unknowable God; Christians believe in a God who is loving and approachable;[22] Jains believe that each person has a potential to become God. The following table is a summary of different traditions.

God/Soul/Body

	Jainism	Christianity	Judaism	Islam	Hinduism	Buddhism
God	Each living being has a Soul. God is a fully enlightened Soul. Each Soul is capable of becoming God	God is loving, creator of heavens and Earth. Holy Spirit and Trinity which guides; to love and show compassion; Yahweh, enduring possibility. Jesus is son of God.	Yahweh, one God, Jehovah, the God of Abraham (Jesus is a false prophet)	Allah – Powerful but unknowable (Jesus was a prophet)	Multitudes of gods but one supreme reality	Theravadas are atheist; Mahayana are polytheistic; Buddha said nothing is permanent.

	Jainism	Christianity	Judaism	Islam	Hinduism	Buddhism
Who created the universe	Matter changes, no one created it. Soul is uncreated and eternal.	God is the creator of heavens and Earth	God	God (Allah)	God	Changing
Purpose of self-human life	To help each other; to realize one's own full potential; To manage one's passions	Faith in Christ; prayer, Bible study	Choose to do good; Bearer of conscious experience-psyche; human means to vie between good and evil desires, so choose the good	To submit to the will of God to gain a Paradise after death. Follow five pillars: faith, prayer, alms, pilgrimage, fasting. Human nature has equal ability to do good or evil.	Attain better rebirth.	Avoid suffering and gain enlightenment
Body and its relation to the Soul/god	Body is matter; Soul is non-matter-energy	Soul resides in body	The body is the repository of the Soul	Not defined.	Two different entities	Two different entities

Actions and Next Life

	Jainism	Christianity	Judaism	Islam	Hinduism	Buddhism
Who controls your actions	We are responsible for our own actions	God and individual's sins.	Human free will, though the total plan is seen by yahweh		God	Self
Meaning of happiness	Compassion, managing your passions	Loving Christ	life = meaning and purpose			

	Jainism	Christianity	Judaism	Islam	Hinduism	Buddhism
Is there a cause/effect	Yes. All thought, speech, and action make an imprint on your Soul (Karma) and their effects are felt throughout your current and future lives	No direct link in this life. God judges at the end.	No direct link in this life. God judges at the end.	No direct link in this life. God judges at the end.	Yes	Yes
Human suffering is due to	Unable to understand our true nature. Attachment to matter/physical realm.	All have sinned and separated from God.	Uncontrollable events; Preventable occurrences		Maya – desire for worldly materials; Humans are in bondage to ignorance and illusion.	Maya – desire for physical material
How to reach Nirvana/salvation	Living a life of Non-Violence, Non-Absolutism, and Non-Possessiveness	Follow Christ's message of love and to believe in Him. For some, sacraments and good work.	Not discussed	Follow Quran	Give up Maya.	
Is there reincarnation/rebirth	Yes until Nirvan/Moksh is attained	No, but after death there is eternal heaven or hell (or temporary purgatory)	Exists only in the mystical tradition	No	Yes	Yes, until enlightenment. No surviving Soul

	Jainism	Christianity	Judaism	Islam	Hinduism	Buddhism
Definition of time, knowledge, universe	Extensive description of this in literature	No	No	No	Yes	Yes

Roots/Origin of Religion

	Jainism	Christianity	Judaism	Islam	Hinduism	Buddhism
Year started	Eternal; 3500 BC, India	30 A.D. Israel	circa 1300 BCE (after destruction of the Second Temple in 70 AD)	622 AD, Saudi Arabia	Eternal	520 BC, India
Key propagator	Rishabhnath, Mahävir (2500 BC)	Jesus Christ	Abraham	Muhammad		Gautama Buddha
Forces which started/ propagated the religion	Violence toward animals and humans	Conditions at the time; Oppression	God communicating with Avram			Observed suffering in day to day life
Number of worldwide followers	10 million	2 billion; 1 out of every 3 individuals	15 million	1.3 billion (Sunni: 940 million)	900 million	360 million
Number of sects	3 major sects	Many	5 or 6	Sunni, Shite, others	Many	Mahayana and Theravada

	Jainism	Christianity	Judaism	Islam	Hinduism	Buddhism
Scriptures, word of God, prophet, belief	Written several hundred years after Mähävir; modified over time	Started 40 years after Christ's death; modified over time	Not modified but interpreted.	Not modified.	Vedas. Modified over time.	Not modified.
Original scriptures versus science today	Strong correlation	Disconnect on creation	May believe in science and god simultaneously		Strong correlation	

Practice

	Jainism	Christianity	Judaism	Islam	Hinduism	Buddhism
Tolerance of other religions	Yes. Respect and understand other faiths	Judaism is true religion, but with incomplete revelation; Islam is false religion.	Islam and Christianity are false interpretations and extensions of Judaism	Jews and Christians are respected but they have wrong beliefs and only partial revelation.	Yes	Yes
Missionary zeal	No	Yes. Send missionaries to other countries.	No reason for missionary work	Yes. Convert to Islam.	No	No
Purpose of prayers	To celebrate the qualities of an enlightened being/Soul	To reach salvation	To enter a dialog with god	Pray to Allah	One with supreme	Self-realization

	Jainism	Christianity	Judaism	Islam	Hinduism	Buddhism
Key scriptures/ writings	Samaysär, Tattvärth-Sutra	The Holy Bible and New Testaments	Torah, N'vi'im, Ketuvim TaNaKh	Quran, Hadith		Tripitaka (Pali Canon); Mahayana sutras like the Lotus Sutras.
Stages in life	Layperson, monks, 14 stages of spiritual progress	Baptism, marriage or Holy Orders, sacraments to the sick	Birth, bar-mitzvah, wedding, death			
Diet	Vegetarian (no meat, fish, eggs); some are vegan; no alcohol.	During lent, or before taking communion some food restrictions or fasting	Kosher foods	No alcohol or pork	Vegetarian	Vegetarian when convenient
Key laypeople vows	Non-Violence, Non-Possessiveness, truth, non-stealing, managing sensual desires	To follow Christ's teachings	That which is hateful to you, do not do to others.			
Key monk vows	Non-Violence, Non-Possessiveness, truth, non-stealing, managing sensual desires	Priests, ministers, pastors, bishops. To give up all possessions.	Rabbis; strict following	Imams		Four noble truths; eightfold path

Religious festivals	Mahävir Jayanti, Paryushan Parv-DasLakshan, Diwali	Christmas, Lent, Easter	Chanukah, High Holidays, Passover, Purim, Shabbat	Ramadan, Eid	Diwali, Holi, Raksha Bandhan	Vesakha, Modlam Chenmo, Assayuja Asalha

JAINISM – A Message to the Interfaith Community

"Ahimsa Parmodharma-Non injury to all living beings." [23]

Jainism is a philosophy, religion, and a way of life that has developed in India over many thousands of years. Jain philosophy is based on the spiritual value of every single living being with the notion that every individual Soul is independent and free to create its own destiny. Jain theory of Karma is "as you sow so should you reap."

Jain tradition is a historical tradition. While the Jain path to freedom comes to us from a remote period in man's history, the most recent Jinas to actually deliver its message to humanity were Lord Parshva (877-777 B.C.E) and Lord Mahävir (599-527 B.C.E). They were not founders of any religion, but only the last of 24 "Crossing-makers," or Tirthankars, great omniscient teachers who lived at various times in the man's cultural history. These Crossing-makers accomplished the highest spiritual goal of existence and then taught their contemporaries the way to reach it by crossing over to the safe shore of spiritual purity. Jainism's core belief is Ahimsa, or non-injury to all living beings.

Lord Mahävir once said, "In happiness and suffering, in joy and grief, we should regard all creatures as we regard our own self." Jainism preaches friendship with all living beings. All Jains are strict vegetarians, consuming only from the plant kingdom.

Jainism is not a sect or part or offshoot of another religion. Jain Religion is the path of Jinas, or "conquerors." A Jin is any person of this world who is a conqueror of his inner enemies, and has subdued the senses, silenced the passions, eliminated every level of attachment, aversion, hate, anger, greed, deceit and worldly desire and thus attained absolute knowledge and peace.

Jains have an important saying: "Non-Violence is the supreme path." The Jain outlook places equal responsibilities on each and every one of us to preserve, protect and help each other, and live in peace and harmony. Jains have a firm conviction that amity between all humanity and life is the true wealth of our planet.

In keeping with the Jain principle of reverence for life, Jains are known for their charitable works, including building shelters for animals. Jainism preaches unconditional universal love, tolerance and compassion for all and does not seek to make converts. There are about 7-10 million Jains in the world today.

"Those who praise their own faith, disparage their opponents and possess malice against them will remain confined to the cycles of birth and death."— Sutrakritaang

[22] Pravin Shah, Jaina Education, Raleigh, NC
[23] Naresh Jain, NJ
Jain Center of Greater Boston – Level 6 Pathshala – Multiplicity of World Religion presentation at JAINA Convention - 2001
http://www.religionfacts.com/islam/comparison_charts/islam_judaism_christianity.htm

Resources

Web Resources

Introduction to Jainism

Jainism: The Basics

These sites offer quick summaries on Jainism and the basic principles.

http://www.jainism.org/m1.html
http://altreligion.about.com/library/faqs/bl_jainism.htm
http://www.bbc.co.uk/religion/religions/jainism/
http://www.angelfire.com/co/jainism/
http://www.jcnc.org/jainism/reference.asp
http://www.jainworld.com/education.htm
http://www.fas.harvard.edu/~pluralsm/affiliates/jainism/index.htm
http://www.jcgb.org

Jain Super sites

These are sites with a large number of articles and books compiled using extensive efforts.

http://www.jainworld.com/
http://www.atmadharma.com/
http://www.terapanth.com/

Jainism for Children

The following web sites for children are fun and exciting:

http://www.jainworld.com/literature/dictionary/alphaframe.htm – Jain Alphabet
http://www.jainworld.com/shortstories/ssindex.htm – Jain Stories
http://www.jainworld.com/teachers/child3.asp – Variety of Jain teaching material
http://www.jainworld.com/education.htm – Guide to teaching Jain School/Pathshala
http://www.jainstudy.org/MoralSt-WhyReligion-1.01.htm – Jain Stories

Intermediate Level Jainism

Jain Prayers

The following web sites have many of the Jain mantras, sutras, and prayers. These prayers are in Hindi with English translation. The meanings of these sacred prayers are also given.

www.jainpujä.com – Excellent site for online streaming pujä with temple graphics

http://www.jainworld.com/bhs/bhsmeang.htm – Bhaktamar Sutra

http://www.cs.colostate.edu/%7Emalaiya/j/divo.html – Aarti and Mangal Dipa

http://www.atmasiddhi.com/book.html – Atma Siddhi

http://www.terapanth.com/popular_mantra.htm – A collection of mantras

Jain Calendar

Jain Calendar is complex. The following link offers a great guide to Jain calendar and festivals.

http://www.cs.colostate.edu/%7Emalaiya/calendar.html

Jain Magazines

The following web sites are links to the popular magazines and back issues.

http://www.jainstudy.org/

http://www.jainworld.com/literature/periodicals/lofjainmag.htm

http://www.jainsamaj.org/magazines/newspage_1.htm

Jain Literature

There are numerous books on Jainism. Some are available here for free download:

http://www.ibiblio.org/jainism/database/BOOK/book.html

http://www.jainworld.com/scriptures/purusharthasiddhyapaya.asp

Jain Pilgrimages

The following links guide you to hundreds of Jain temples and pilgrimages (Tirthsthans).

http://www.jaintirth.org

http://www.pilgrimage-india.com/jain-pilgrimage/

http://www.jainsamaj.org/ – Along with excellent information about several temples, this web site offers biographical information about Jain priests, and a matrimonial database.

http://www.jaintirthdarshan.com

Audio: Jain Sutras and Lectures

These web sites provide hundreds of lectures and sutras in audio format.

http://www.jainworld.net/realaudvdo/divdhwani/divdhwani1.htm

http://jainworld.com/lectures/mixed.asp

Jain Discussions

If you are interested in discussing Jainism, the following web sites are for you. Many engaging and interesting discussions, all about Jainism, happen here.

http://groups.yahoo.com/group/jainlist/

http://groups.yahoo.com/group/jain-friends/

http://groups.yahoo.com/group/Jain_Pictures/

Jain Organizations

Would you like to be more involved in Jainism? Along with visiting your local Jain Centers, you can also join the various Jain organizations in your area.

Federation of Jain Associations in North America

www.jaina.org

www.jwol.org

JAINA is the main Jain organization in North America with over 60 Jain centers and 30 subcommittees. JAINA's vision is to Live and Share a Jain Way of Life.

Young Jain Professionals

The Young Jain Professionals is a group of people who focus on increasing the awareness and understanding of Jainism amongst the Jain working professionals in North America. www.yjponline.org

Young Jains of America

This organization is for Young Jains. They hold a convention once every two years.
www.yja.org

Young Jains of Singapore

www.sjrs.org.sg

Young Jains UK

www.youngjains.org.uk

Jains in Australia

http://jains.australians.com

Other Resources:

http://www.shubhlabh.net/usatemples.html
http://www.garamchai.com/jains.htm
http://en.wikipedia.org/wiki/Jain_Community_Associations/_Study_Centres_in_the_West
http://www.pluralism.org/directory/results.php?sort=state%2Ccity%2Ctitle&tradition=Jain

Intermediate & Special Interest Sites

Books: You can search university libraries, web-based booksellers and some lists:
http://catalog.loc.gov/
http://www.jaindharam.org/List of Printed Jain Books in English.htm
http://www.hindibooks.8m.com/

http://www.mlbd.com/
http://members.tripod.com/malaiya/shravak.html (amazon.com)

Rituals and Symbols: Ritual descriptions and symbolism can be found here:
http://www.ibiblio.org/jainism/database/RITUAL/ritual.html
http://www.cs.colostate.edu/~malaiya/om.html

Images: You can find free clip-art at
http://www.cs.colostate.edu/~malaiya/jainclip.html
Many beautiful images can be seen at
http://www.jainworld.com/pictures/jpcindex.htm
http://groups.yahoo.com/group/Jain_Pictures/

Glossaries:
http://www.cs.colostate.edu/~malaiya/jaingloss.htm

Jain Names: There is even a list of Jain baby names:
http://jainfriends.faithweb.com/

Advanced

Texts: Some excellent sources for scholarly books and articles are here:
http://www.terapanth.com/impressions/index.htm
http://www.sendai-ct.ac.jp/~ousaka/1109F/Win95down.html/ (original texts)
http://www.jainworld.com/jainbooks/bookslist.htm
http://www.jinvani.com/
http://www.angelfire.com/co/atmajyoti/
http://jainfriends.faithweb.com/
http://www.ibiblio.org/jainism/database/JAINEDU/jainedu.html

1. http://www.cs.colostate.edu/~malaiya/jainhlinks.html
2. http://www.jainism.free-online.co.uk/
3. http://www.umich.edu/~umjains/jainismsimplified/jainsimp.html
4. http://www.religioustolerance.org/jainism.htm
5. http://www.jainworld.com/

Jainism: Jain Principles, Traditions, Practices

www.cs.colostate.edu/~malaiya/jainhlinks.html

This Jain web site has an easy-to-use links section which contains links to several articles and other Jain resources.

Harvard Pluralism Project

http://www.pluralism.org/pluralism/what_is_pluralism.php
www.jainstudy.org

One of the most comprehensive resources on world religion including Jainism.

Jain Study Circle

www.jainstudy.org

A magazine containing articles, stories, and poems on Jainism and related subjects.

Jainworld

www.jainworld.com

Jainworld is an excellent web site that provides educational information, literature, recipes and a lot more.

Jain Center of Greater Boston

www.jcgb.org

A refreshed web site with links to many resources.

Jain Society of Northern California

www.jcnc.org

A user-friendly web site that provides visitors with several resources.

Essence of Jainism

http://www.atmadharma.com

This web site has a variety of topics covered in terms of Jainism. This web site also offers educational information based on knowledge level.

Atma-Siddhi

www.atmasiddhi.com

Has information about Shrimad Rajchandraji and the Atma-Siddhi.

Jainnet

www.jainnet.com

Excellent site to visit for an introduction to Jainism, lyrics, recipes, and ecards.

Vegetarianism Sites

The following web sites focus on vegetarianism and delicious vegetarian recipes. Note that not all vegetarian recipes are suitable for Jains who have taken higher Vrats (vows).

Vegetarianism & Ahimsa: There are many excellent sites like
http://www.ivu.org/
http://www.bawarchi.com/cookbook/jain.html
http://www.veggiefiles.com/dir/not_alone/meatheads/24.php
http://www.wizard.net/~ethan/ahimsa.html
http://vegweb.com/
http://vegkitchen.com/
http://www.veggiecooking.com/
http://www.nanday.com/cookbook/

Veggies Unite

http://www.vegweb.com/

Veggies Unite provides information on vegetarianism and includes vegetarian recipes, a discussion board, and many articles may provide valuable information.

Vegetarianism in a Nutshell

www.vrg.org/nutshell/nutshell.htm

Offers details about being a vegetarian, as well as specifics regarding vitamins and simple food substitutions.

Vegan

www.vegan.org

Promotes people choosing the vegan food habits, and provides vegans with information about what to eat for meals.

Vegan Essentials

www.veganessentials.com

Focuses on vegan products ranging from food, clothing, and vitamins.

Go Veg

www.goveg.com

This is a PETA site that provides information about health, activist kits and information on animal rights.

Animal Cruelty and Ahimsa

People for the Ethical Treatment of Animals

www.peta.org

PETA is one of the leaders in promoting animal rights. Extensive information is available on this topic.

The American Society For the Prevention of Cruelty to Animals

http://www.aspca.org

The ASPCA is another organization that urges the prevention of cruelty to animals. This site offers information about adopting animals as well as pet nutrition and national shelter outreaches.

Ahimsa of Texas

www.ahimsatx.org/

Ahimsa of Texas is an organization promoting kindness to all life, with the primary focus on eliminating the euthanasia of healthy animals in our community shelters and animal pounds.

Ahimsa: The Real Right to Live Movement

www.wizard.net/~ethan/Source-Of-Peace.htm

This Ahimsa site offers religious perspectives from various other groups.

If you come across other web sites that we should include in the next edition of this book, please send email to jwolhandbook@ yahoo.com.

"Thou shalt not kill." — Exodus 20:13 (The Bible)

Cruelty-Free Products

Below is a sample list of the cruelty-free items that were researched by 7th and 8th grade Jain Pathshala students:

Product Name	Where to Buy
Category: Cosmetics/Daily Use Merchandise (Not Tested On Animals)	
Liquid Glycerin Soap	Trader Joe's
Extra Dry Formula Moisturizer	Trader Joe's
Refresh Citrus Shampoo & Refresh Citrus Conditioner	Trader Joe's
Nourish Spa Shampoo & Nourish Spa Conditioner	Trader Joe's
Tom's Toothpaste – Various Flavors	Trader Joe's
Flirt Eye Shadow	Kohl's
Tresemme Shampoo	Kohl's
Botanical Shampoo	Kohl's
LA Looks Hair Gel	General Grocery or Drug Store
L'Oreal Kids Shampoo	General Grocery or Drug Store
St. Ives Lotion	General Grocery or Drug Store
Bath & Body – Shower Gel	Bath & Body Works*
Cucumber-Melon Hand Lotion	Bath & Body Works*
Sweet Pea Handmade Soap	Bath & Body Works*
Organic Citrus Perfume	Icing/Claire's
Avon-Moisture 24 Cream	Avon.com*

Product Name	Where to Buy
Category: Jain Food Items (No Meat, Eggs, Honey, Gelatin or Underground Vegetables)	
Pillsbury Muffin Mix	General Grocery Store
Pillsbury Waffles Homestyle – Frozen	General Grocery Store
Pillsbury Moist Supreme Classic Yellow Premium Cake Mix	General Grocery Store
Aunt Jemima "The Original" Pancake & Waffle Mix	General Grocery Store
Kraft South Beach Diet High Protein Cereal Bars	General Grocery Store
Ghiradelli Chocolates	General Grocery Store
Teddy Grahams Snacks – Chocolate or Cinnamon	General Grocery Store
Air Heads Fruit Spinners	General Grocery Store
Boston Cookies – Vegan – Various Flavors	Whole Foods
Egg-less Chocolate Cake	Some local bakers offer this
Vegan Chocolate Cake	Whole Foods
Asiago Peppercorn Bread	Trader Joe's
Raisin Bread and Light Wheat Bread	Roche Bros.

*All products of this company are not tested on animals.

> *"I say with conviction that the doctrine for which the name of Lord Mahaveer is glorified nowadays is the doctrine of Ahimsa.*
> *If anyone has practiced to the fullest extent and has propagated most the doctrine of Ahimsa, it was Lord Mahāvir."*
> — Mahatma Gandhi

Source: Jain Center of Boston Pathshala children (teacher: Preeti Jain)

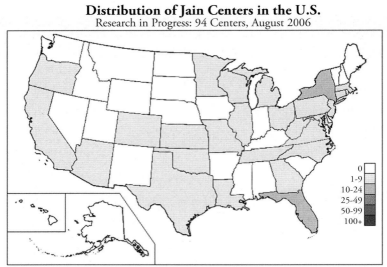

Distribution of Jain Centers in the U.S.
Research in Progress: 94 Centers, August 2006

0
1-9
10-24
25-49
50-99
100+

Source – The Pluralism Project at Harvard University: Directory of Religious Centers © 2006
http://www.pluralism.org/directory

Jain Centers and Societies

As Jainism continues to spread through the country, Jains look for places to practice their way of life with others who share their beliefs. However, they sometimes have trouble finding a derasar or temple to go to, whether they have just moved to a new house, just want to get more involved in a temple, or would like to visit a temple while on vacation. The following is a listing of temples and Jain associations throughout the United States along with contact information, organized alphabetically by state.

Name	Web site	Address	Contact Number
Jain Center of Greater Phoenix	www.jcgp.org	P.O. Box 64221 Phoenix, Arizona 85082	602-863-1073
Jain Center of Northern California	www.jcnc.org	722 South Main Street, Milpitas, California 95035	408-262-6242
Jain Center of Southern California	www.jaincenter.net	8072 Commonwealth Avenue, P.O. Box 549, Buena Park, California 90621	714-739-9161

Name	Web site	Address	Contact Number
Jain Society of Greater Sacramento	None	5239 Fair Oaks Boulevard, Carmichael, California 95608	916-488-2601
Jain Society of San Diego	None	9185 Westvale Road, San Diego, California 92129	858-676-1150
Jain Center of Connecticut	None	7 Trailling Ridge Road, Brookfield, Connecticut 06805	203-775-1906
Jain Center of Greater Hartford	None	23 Fellen Road, Storrs, Connecticut 06268	860-487-0607
Jain Center of Colorado	None	10976 West 66th Avenue, Arvada, Colorado 80004	303-420-7049
Arun Jain Inter-Cultural		233 North Ocean Ave. Daytona Beach, Florida 32018	
Jain Association of Northeast Florida	None	1832 St. Lawrence Way, Jacksonville, Florida 32223	904-273-4124
Jain Association of Palm Beach and Treasure Coast		3949 Whaleboat Way Wellington, Florida 33414	561-793-3564
Jain Center of Fort Myers	None	6759 Highland Pines Circle, Fort Myers, Florida 33912	239-561-2731
Jain Center of South Florida	None	10135 SW, 144th Pl., Miami, Florida 33186	954-885-9579
Jain Society Inc. of Tampa Bay	None	25350 U.S. 19 N., Apt. # 6 Clearwater, Florida 34263	727-781-8036
Jain Society of Central Florida, Inc.	www.jsocf.org	407 West Citrust Street, Altamonte Springs, Florida 32714	407-323-3509

Name	Web site	Address	Contact Number
Jain Society of Southern Florida	None	6100 Old Winter Garden Road, Orlando, Florida 32835	407-295-8694
Jain Vishwa Bharati	www.jainvishwabharati.org	7819 Lillwill Avenue, Orlando, Florida 32809	407-852-8694
Augusta Jain Community		408 Hastings Place Martinez, Georgia 30907	706-863-6976
Hindu Temple Society of Augusta (Hindu/Jain Temple)	www.augustahts.org	1421 Luke Road, Augusta, Georgia 30907	706-860-3864
Jain Group of Atlanta	None	1281 Cooper Lake Road, Smyrna, Georgia 30082	404-469-7385
Jain Society of Greater Atlanta	www.jsgatemple.org	669 South Peachtree Rd. Norcross, Georgia 30071	404-325-0627
Jain Society of Metropolitan Chicago	www.jsmc.org	435 North Rt. 59, Barlett, Illinois 60103	708-837-1077
Jain Society of Kansas City		15404, W-79th Terrace Lenexa, Kansas 66219	913-599-4582
Jain Center of Southern Louisiana	None	3829 Deer Creek Lane, Harvey, Louisiana 70058	504-340-4283
Jain Society of Metropolitan Washington	www.jainsocietydc.org	1021 Briggs Cheney Road, Silver Springs, Maryland 20905	703-620-9837
Jain Center of Greater Boston	www.jcgb.org	15 Cedar Street, Norwood, Massachusetts 02062	781-762-9490
Jain Sangh of New England	www.jsne.org	124-A Cummings Park Drive, Woburn, Massachusetts 01801	781-245-0051

Name	Web site	Address	Contact Number
Jain Society of Greater Detroit	www.jain-temple.org	29278 W. 12 Mile Road, Farmington Hills, Michigan 48334	248-851-5246
Jain Society of Greater Lansing	None	1047 Prescott Street, East Lansing, Michigan 48823	517-203-0888
Jain Center of Minnesota	www.jaincentermn.org	147 14th Avenue SW, St. Paul, Minnesota 55112	952-445-8581
Jain Center of Greater St. Louis	www.jcstl.org	725 Weldman Road, St. Louis, Missouri 63011	636-230-3300
Jain Study Center of North Carolina (Raleigh)	www.jainism.org	309 Ariation Parkway, Morrisville, North Carolina 27560	919-469-0956
Jain Study Group of Charlotte	None	7400 City View Drive, Charlotte, North Carolina 28212	704-535-3440
Jain Center of New Jersey	www.jaincenternj.org	233 Runnymede Road, Essex Falls, New Jersey 07021	908-329-3236
Jain Sangh of Pennsylvania, New Jersey, and Delaware	www.jainsangh.org	3401 Cooper Avenue Pennsauken, New Jersey 08109	856-662-2627
Jain Vishva Bharati of North America	www.jvbna.org/	151 Middlesex Ave Iselin, New Jersey 08830	
Siddhachalam/International Mahävir Jain Mission	www.siddhachalam.org	65 Mud Pond Road, Blaristown, New Jersey, 07825	908-362-9793
The Jain Sangh of New Jersey	None	3401 Cooper Avenue, Pennsauken, New Jersey 08109	609-567-2331

Name	Web site	Address	Contact Number
Jain Association of Elmira		108 Lincoln Road Horseheads, New York 14845	607-796-9065
Jain Center of America	www.nyjaincenter.org	43-11 Ithaca Street, Elmhurst, New York 11373	718-478-9141
Jain Center of Syracuse	None	4013 Pawnee Drive, Liverpool, New York 13090	305-622-3287
Jain Meditation International Center (JMIC)		401 East 86th Street #20A New York, New York 10028	212-362-6483
Jain Sangh of Hudson Valley		18 Stephen Drive Hopewell Junction, New York 14533	914-226-6016
Jain Society of Buffalo	None	1560 North French Road, Crefzille, New York 14068	716-634-7469
Jain Society of Capital District, Albany NY	None	450 Albany-Shaker Road, Loudonville, New York 12211	518-785-7470
Jain Society of Long Island	None	614 Woodbury Road, Plainview, New York 11803	516-942-0258
Jain Society of Rochester	None	14 Ambergate Rise, Pittsford, New York 14534	716-264-9834
JAINA – Federation of Jain Associations in North America	www.jaina.org	P.O. Box 700 Getzville, New York 14068	716-636-5342
Jain Society of Las Vegas	www.hindutemplelv.org	1701 Sageberry Drive, Las Vegas, Nevada 89144	702-304-9207
Jain Center of Central Ohio	www.jcoco.org	2770 Sawbury Blvd., Columbus, Ohio 43225	614-596-7887

Name	Web site	Address	Contact Number
Jain Center of Central Ohio	www.jcoco.org	91 S. Ireland Blvd. Mansfield, Ohio 44906	
Jain Center of Cincinnati and Dayton	None	6798 Cincinnati-Dayton Road, Cincinnati, Ohio 45044	513-885-7414
Jain Center of Toledo		7219 Cloister Road Toledo, Ohio 43617	419-841-8985
Jain Society of Greater Cleveland	www.jsgc.org	14835 Lancelot Lane, North Royalton, Ohio 44138	440-748-3420
Tulsa Jain Sangh		8707 E. 133rd Place Bixby, Oklahoma 74008	918-369-3163
Jain Society of Oregon	None	5432 S.W. Seymour Street, Portland, Oregon 97221	503-292-1965
Hindu Jain Center of Pittsburgh	www.hindujaintemple.org	615 Illini Drive, Monroeville, Pennsylvania 15146	724-325-2054
Jain Center of South Central PA		301 Stelgerwalt Hallo Rd. Philadelphia, Pennsylvania 17070	717-898-6173
Jain Sangh of Allentown	None	4200 Airport Road, Allentown, Pennsylvania 18130	610-868-1231
Jain Society of Pittsburgh	None	1010 Summer Ridge Court, Murrysville, Pennsylvania 15668	724-327-6570
Samarpan Hindu/Jain Temple	www.samarpantemple.org	6515 Bustleton Avenue Philadelphia, Pennsylvania 19149	215-537-9537

Name	Web site	Address	Contact Number
Samarpan Jain Sangh, Inc		9701 Bustleton Avenue Philadelphia, Pennsylvania 19115	215-464-7676
Jain Group of Greenville	None	108 Meaway Court, Simsonville, South Carolina 92681	803-9674605
Jain Society of Middle Tennessee	None	2273 Pewitt Drive, Clarksville, Tennessee 37403	931-648-9535
Jain Society of Greater Memphis	None	2173 East Glendalen Drive, Memphis, Tennessee 38139	901-755-3600
Jain Center of West Texas	None	1110 Juneau Avenue, Lubbock, Texas 79416	409-295-1600
Jain Society of Houston	www.jain-houston.org	3905 Arc Street, Houston, Texas 77215	713-789-2338
Jain Society of North Texas	www.dfwjains.org	538 Apollo Road, Richardson, Texas 75081	972-470-0606
Jain Vishwa Bharati Institute Preksha Meditation Center – Houston		1712 Highway 6 South Houston, Texas 77077	281-596-9642
Jainova (Jains of Northern Virginia)	www.jainova.org/index.html	3728 Persimmon Circle Fairfax, Virgina 22031	
Jain Religion Center of Wisconsin	www.jainwi.org	N4063 W243 Pewaukee Rd. Highway 164 North, Pewaukee, Wisconsin 53072	262-242-0245
Prerana Yoga & Meditation Foundation		1302 Deer Run Morgantown, Wyoming 26505	304-594-1818

http://www.shubhlabh.net/usatemples.html
http://www.jaina.org/about/centerpresidents.asp
http://www.garamchai.com/jains.htm
http://en.wikipedia.org/wiki/Jain_Community_Associations/_Study_Centres_in_the_West
http://www.jainworld.com
http://www.pluralism.org/directory/results.php?sort=state%2Ccity%2Ctitle&tradition=Jain

Glossary of Non-English Jain Terms

Abhavya	One who is incapable of attaining moksha.
Abhigrah	Resolution.
Abhishek	Anointing ceremony.
Achaksurdarshan	Perception by means of the senses other than visual.
Ächarya/ji	A Sädhu who learned, mastered and taught religious scriptures, follows them, and is now the head of a Sangh. Head of a mendicant group, spiritual leader and monk-scholar.
Adhi	Two and a half.
Adho-lok	The lower world. The home of infernal beings.
Ägama	Scripture. Canonical literature.
Aghati	The four types of Karmas whose powers are much milder than those of the four ghati Karmas. These Karmas end at the end of a life.
Agni	Fire.
Ahimsa	Non-violence, non-harming. The supreme mahavrat or anuvrat that all Jains must adhere to. Jain religion is remarkable in that it upholds non-violence as the supreme religion (Ahimsa Paramo Dharm) and has insisted upon its observance in thought, word, and deed at the individual as well as social levels.
Ahimsa Paramo Dharma	"Non-violence is the supreme religion."
Ailak	The highest state of a Digambar layman, wherein he retains only one piece of clothing.
Akäsh	Space.
Alok-äkäsh	Totally empty space.

Amari	Prohibition of animal sacrifice.
Anekäntväd	"Non-singular conclusively" or multiplicity of viewpoints. The concept that humans, with obstructed knowledge, will only be able to see limited parts of any whole (situation or truth).
Antaräy	A Ghati Karma that obstructs the strength of a Soul.
Anuvrat	A vow that is not as strict as a mahavrat. Anuvrats are for people living family lives. The five Vrats are Ahimsa (non-violence), truth, non-stealing, non-possessiveness and chastity or self-control.
Aparigraha	Non-possessiveness. One of the mahavrats and anuvrats.
Ärä	One of the six divisions of time in one half of the time cycle. Runs from thousands to billions of years. We are currently in the fifth ara of the descending half of the time cycle, which started some 2,500 years ago.
Arambhi-himsä	Violence occurring either accidentally or through the performance of an acceptable occupation.
Arati	The lamp-waving ceremony.
Arihant	Conqueror of internal enemies, such as anger, pride, deceit, greed, jealousy, hatred, intrigue and various other passions.
Äsrav	Karmic influx. One of the nine tattvas.
Asteya	Non-stealing. One of the mahavrats and anuvrats.
Atishay	Thirty-four special attributes of Tirthankars.
Atithi	One who may come any time, unexpectedly, without invitation, and is still welcomed with love and respect.
Ätma	Soul.
Avamaudarya	Eating only a very small portion of food.
Avarsarpini	Regressive half of the time cycle.
Äyu Karma	Karma that determines the span of a given lifetime.
Ayushya	An aghati Karma that determines how long you will live.
Bandh	Karmic bondage. One of the nine tattvas.
Beindriy	Souls that live with two senses, namely touch and taste.
Bhante	Respected (Lord).
Bharat	Name of a kshetra. We live in Bharat Kshetra. It is located in the southern part of Jambu Dweep (look at geography section for more details).
Bhäv	Internal. States of a dravya. Thoughts, contemplations.
Bhoga-antäray	Karma that restricts enjoyment.

Brahmacharya	Physical control, abstinence, chastity. One of the mahavrats and anuvrats. Jainism emphasizes abstinence from over-indulgence, voluntary curtailment of one's needs, and the consequent subsiding of the aggressive urge. For shrävaks and shrävikas, this also means remaining sexually monogamous to one's own spouse. For sädhus and sädhvis this entails strict abstinence.
Brahmacharya-ashrama	The life of a student. The first of four stages that a Jain shrävak and shrävika are recommended to pass through in his or her lifetime.
Charitra	Conduct.
Chattari	Four.
Chauvisattho	A prayer to the 24 Tirthankars of this kaal in Bharat Kshetra. We bow and praise them for their great virtues.
Chaurindriy	Soul that lives with four senses, namely touch, taste, smell and sight.
Chauvisi	A group of 24.
Dän	Charity. Alms-giving.
Däna-antaräy	A type of Karma that hinders the practice of charity.
Darshan	Vision. Intuition. Insight. Perception. A system of philosophy. A pure Soul has infinite vision.
Darshanävaraniya	A ghati Karma that obstructs the capacity of a Soul to see things clearly.
Dev	A Soul in heaven, or at a high spiritual level.
Dev-dushya	"Divine" cloth. A finely woven piece of cloth.
Devlok	Heaven. The place where devs reside.
Dhairya	Patience. A pure Soul has infinite patience.
Dharma	Holy law. Righteousness (ten forms).
Dharma dravya	The principle of motion.
Dharma tirtha	Holy path.
Dhivyadhvani	Miraculous sound. When a Tirthankar attains enlightenment, this sound emerges from them, silent, yet understood by every living being in his or her own language.
Digambar	Sky-clad. Name of the Jaina sect whose mendicants (munis) practice ascetic nudity.
Dravya	Substance.
Dukkadam	Forgive me (or dissolve my mistakes).
Dweep	Island. A large isolated area. There are two and a half dweeps, each with three kshetras in them.
Ek	One; unitary.
Ekäntaväd	Extremism. Absolutist doctrine.

Eka satak	A mendicant who wears a single piece of cloth.
Ekendriy	A being with only one sense faculty, that of touch. A synonym for sthavara beings.
Ganadhara/ji	The first mendicant disciples of Tirthankars. Supporters of the order. Mahävir had 11, the most famous of which was Gautamswami.
Ghäti	The four types of Karmas, whose powers are much stronger than those of the aghati Karmas. Karmas that have a vitiating effect upon the qualities of the Soul. These powers may last for many lives.
Gäan (jnän)	Knowledge. A pure Soul has infinite knowledge.
Gnanavaraniy	A ghati Karma that obstructs the capacity of the Soul to know things in their purest forms.
Gotra Karma	Karmas that determine environmental circumstances.
Gruhasth-ashrama	Family life. The second of four stages that a Jain shrävak and shrävika are recommended to pass through in his or her lifetime.
Gunasthana	The 14 stages of purification.
Gunavrats	Retraints that reinforce the practice of anuvratas.
Himsa	Injury, harming, violence.
Hundavasarpini	A period of avasarpini in which extraordinary events may take place.
Indriya	Sense organ.
Jaina	Followers of a Jina, a synonym for Nigantha.
Jain-brahman	Laypeople in charge of priestly functions within certain Jaina communities.
Jambu dweep	"The continent of the rose-apple tree." The realm in the universe that is inhabited by humans. This region is transversed by six mountains which divide the region into seven regions. The most important regions are India in the south, Airavat in the north, and Mahavideha in the middle. It is believed that in these three regions, humans may find rewards for religious pursuits and that deliverance may be possible.
Janma-kalyän	Birth. One of the five auspicious events in the career of a Tirthankar.
Jin	"Conqueror." He who has conquered love and hate, pleasure and pain, attachment and aversion, and has thereby freed his Soul from the Karmas obscuring knowledge, perception, truth, and ability, is a Jina. The Jains refer to the Jin as God.
Jin-ägam	Jaina scripture.
Jina-bhavan	Jaina temple.
Jiv	Soul.
Jiva Dayä	Compassion toward living beings.
Jyotish Chakra	Area of space in which zodiac planets, stars, etc. are located.

Käl	Time. Time stages within the progressive and regressive half-cycles. Runs into more than billions of years, per cycle.
Kalyanaka	Auspicious moments.
Karemi	"I do."
Karma	Action. A deed, good or bad. A form of matter. Upon maturing, it delivers its fruit. There are four Ghati and four Aghati types of Karmas. Powers of Ghati Karmas are much stronger, and they last for many lives.
Kashäy	Passion.
Kausagga	A motionless state of body, as if the Soul has departed from it.
Käyotsarg	Abandonment of the body, a standing or sitting posture of meditation.
Kevaldarshan	Infinite vision and perception. After acquiring it, the cycle of births and deaths is broken forever. Any Soul can attain it, by getting rid of Karmas, attachments and hatreds. With it comes kevalgnan, infinite Dhariya, Tapa and Veerya.
Kevaldarshi	One who has kevalgnan.
Kevalgnan	Infinite knowledge. Knowledge isolated from karmic obstruction. Omniscience. Knowledge involving awareness of every existent in all its qualities and modes.
Kevalin/gnani	One who has kevalgnan. Synonym for arhat or omniscient.
Khamana	Homages, or salutations.
Khamasamano	Forgiving Gurudev.
Krodh	Anger.
Kshamä	Forgiveness.
Kshetra	An area, site or location where humans exist. Each kshetra has four more similar counterparts.
Kshullak	Minor. A junior monk. A Jain layman on the eleventh pratima. One who wears three pieces of clothing.
Logassa	(Masters) of the entire universe.
Loguttama	Supreme.
Mahäräj Saheb	"King, sir." A title used for sädhus, to indicate respect.
Mahävideh	Name of a kshetra. Twenty Tirthankars currently exist there, deeming it the most sacred kshetra.

Mahävir	Twenth-fourth Tirthankar in this ara of the time cycle. His name means "The most courageous one." Mahävir lived some time between 599-527 BCE. He was a contemporary of another great spiritual teacher, Gautama Sakyamuni, who would come to be known in history as Buddha. According to most accounts, Mahävir was also a high-born member of a warrior caste who renounced the world when he was 30 to pursue a life as an ascetic. His moment of enlightenment came after 12 years of spiritual pursuit. He then gathered 12 disciples around him, and it is through these disciples that his teachings were eventually documented and disseminated.
Mahävrat	A vow that is much stricter than an Anuvrat. Only those who take diksha will take on these vows (i.e. sädhus and sädhvis). There are five mahavrats, namely, ahimsa, anekantvad, aparigraha, asteya and brahmacharya.
Mangal/ Mangalam	Destroyer of sins. Auspicious.
Mantra	A prayer with strong psychological powers.
Maun	Silence.
Michchhami	"I wish."
Mohaniy	A ghati Karma that obstructs the capacity of Soul to think properly.
Moksha	The state of freedom for a Soul from the cycle of birth and death.
Muktishila (Siddha-shila)	The topmost area of the universe, the area of freedom. After death, a liberated Soul rises to it, and never comes back into the cycle of birth and death. For every Soul that exists there is Kevalgnani, Kevaldarshi and has infinite dhariya, tapa and veerya.
Muni	Monk. Sadhu. One who keeps maun. He only observes, without praising or complaining.
Näm	An aghati Karma that determines the body.
Namotthunam	Expression of respect to the virtuous gurus.
Namaskär mantra (Namokar mantra)	Reverent salutation to the five holy beings: arihants, siddhas, acharyas, upadhayas and sädhus/sädhvis. A prayer consisting of nine lines, which is the most meaningful of all Jain prayers in that it allows the follower to pay homage to all teachers.
Näraki	Hell beings.
Nigod	The lowest form of life.
Nirjarä	Dissociation of Karma. One of the nine tattvas.
Nitya	Eternal.
Niyati	Fate.
Niyativada	Fatalism.

Om	Sacred sound formed by combining the first syllables of five supreme beings (AAAUM) in the namaskär mantra.
Pachchakhan	Formality for taking a vow.
Pad	Poem.
Panch	Five.
Panch kalyan	The five auspicious events in the life of a Tirthankar.
Panchendriy	Souls with five senses, namely touch, taste, smell, sight and hearing.
Pani patra	Hand-bowl. Folding palms to form a bowl for accepting food.
Pannato	Spoken, or taught.
Päp	Unwholesome Karmas.
Paramänu	Atom.
Paramätman	The highest liberated Soul.
Parasparopagraho Jivänam	"Souls render service to one another." From Tattvärtha Sutra 1: 4: 1.
Parva	Jaina holy days.
Parigrahatyäga-pratimä	The ninth stage in which a layman abandons the cares of worldly possessions.
Paryushan-parva	Eight or ten days of holy period for spiritual upliftment, undersanding the qualities of the Soul, prayers, and fasting. Takes place during the rainy season (usually August or September).
Pavajjhami	"I seek."
Phal	Fruit.
Paushadh	A day chosen by a householder to live like a muni.
Pratikraman	Going back to the original virtues (of Soul), which are: compassion, peace, even-temperament, forgiveness, etc.
Pratimä	Stages of renunciation for a layman.
Pudgal	Matter.
Pujä	Worship.
Pundarik	The best lotus.
Punya Karma	Wholesome, good, virtuous, Karma.
Purän	Name of a class of sacred texts dealing with the lives of Tirthankars.

Purva	A group of fourteen Jaina canonical texts, now extinct.
Pushkarvar	Name of a dweep. Only half of it is used for living.
Räg	Desire. Passion. Attachment.
Rajlok / Lok	Geographical term. The universe is divided into 14 rajloks, consisting of hells, dweeps, heavens, etc.
Sädhu/sahoo	A male who has given up the family life, wealth and worldly comforts to seek liberation. He learns scriptures religiously.
Sädhvi/ji	A female who has given up the family life, wealth and worldly comforts to seek liberation.
Samlekhanä	Voluntary and controlled fasting to death. This is a misunderstood and controversial concept in Jainism. It is believed that in 420 BCE, Mahävir engaged in samlekhanä.
Sämäyik	State of calmness and sinlessness of mind and speech. Usually 48 minutes for householders and a lifetime for sädhus and sädhvis.
Samiti	Five areas of caution: walking, speaking, eating food, handling materials and discarding excretion.
Samkit	Awakening of the Soul to the right path. Once a Soul has samkit, he gets liberated within a few incarnations.
Samurchchhin	A small human-like life, of bacterial size, residing inside our human bodies. It can be born spontaneously, by itself.
Samavasaran	Holy assembly of the Jina.
Samay	Moment.
Samkalpaja-himsa	Intentional, premeditated violence.
Samsär	Cycle of transmigration for all non-liberated souls.
Samvar	Stoppage of the influx of Karmas. One of the nine tattvas.
Sangh	Fourfold society, consisting of male and female sädhus and householders who follow the principles of Jainism. Establishing a sangh is what distinguishes a regular kevali from a Tirthankar (a kevali who establishes a sangh).
Santhära	Peaceful, voluntary and planned religious death.
Sanvibhäg	Sharing equally, with love and respect.
Sanyäs-äshram	Life as a monk, a period of renunciation. This is the fourth of four stages that a Jain shrävak and shrävika are recommended to pass through in his or her lifetime.
Sharanam	Shelter.
Shikshävrat	Four vows, which prepare and train a householder for the eventual muni life.
Shrävak/ji	Male householder, following the principles of Jainism.

Shrävika	Female householder, following the principles of Jainism.
Shri	A prefix used to indicate respect.
Siddha	One who has achieved complete liberation from cycles of births and deaths, and now in siddha shila (muktishila).
Stavara	Immobile beings, such as plants.
Sthäpanä	Ritual act of asking a monk to stop for alms.
Sutra	A scripture written in the ancient Ardhamaghdhi language.
Shvetämbar	Name of a Jain sect whose medicants wear white garments.
Tap	Penance which contributes to the destruction of Karmas. A pure Soul has infinite tapa.
Tass	For (my blemished Soul).
Tattva	The nine "reals," regarded as objects of faith for a Jains.
Teindriya	Lives with three senses, namely touch, taste and smell.
Tikhkhuto	Three times.
Tirthankar	"Builders of the ford." One who reestablishes the religion and fourfold society system of Sädhus, Sädhvis, Shrävaks and Shrävikas.
Upädhyäy/ji	A sädhu who learned, mastered and now teaches religious scriptures.
Uttari	Upliftment or elevation.
Vanaprasth-äshrama	Family and service to society. This is the third of four stages that a Jain shrävak and shrävika are recommended to pass through in his or her lifetime.
Vanasi	Forest dweller.
Vandan	Act of bowing, or offering salutations.
Vandanä	Reverent salutation.
Varna	Caste, hierarchy, class. Color. A quality of matter.
Vedaniya	An aghati Karma that determines the mundane experience of pain and pleasure.
Veerya	Strength. A pure Soul has infinite strength.
Vir-nirväna	Beginning of the Jain era. Death anniversary of Mahävir.
Viträg	One who has no attachment.
Vrat	Vow.
Yathapravratta-karana	The Soul's ineradicable tendency toward spiritual growth.

Yati	A spiritually advanced layman of the Svetambara sect.
Yatra	Pilgrimage.
Yog	Vibration, activities.
Yoga	Meditation.
Yojana	A measure of distance equal to about eight or nine miles.

These terms have been compiled from the following sources:

- http://www.yja.org/education/glossary.html
- http://www.ops.org/scrtec/india/jainism.html
- http://www.csupomona.edu/~plin/ews430/jain2.html
- Jaini, Padmanabh S. *The Jaina Path of Purification*. Motilal Banarsidass, Delhi: 1979.
- Jain Center of Southern California, Winter Camp 1991 Information Packet.

"One day the world will look upon research on animals as it now looks upon research on human beings." — Leonardo Da Vinci

?

Questions on Jainism

The following are some common questions asked about Jainism. Visit these sites for responses to these and more questions and responses.

http://www.geocities.com/haren_shah
http://www.jcnc.org/jainism/qa_vow.htm
http://www.yja.org/education/faq/

1. In which book is Jain philosophy described?

2. What is religion?

3. How old is the Jain religion? What is the proof of its existence? What is nature and how does it relate to Jain religion?

4. What is the relationship between the Hindu and Jain Religions?

5. How does the theory of which came first, the "chicken or the egg" fit in the Jain religion?

6. Science has proved that there is a life in the plant. Then, how can we eat vegetables and fruits?

7. If Jains believe in the Non-Violence, than how can we eat milk, butter, cheese etc.? What about the grocery and food manufacturing plant etc.?

8. Jains believe in not killing anyone. a) Suppose you are in a desert and dying of hunger and you see a dead animal. Can you eat that meat to survive? b) You go to a grocery store and are passing by the meat section. You know that meat is already there. If you don't buy it, someone else will buy and eat, or it will decay. What's wrong in buying readily available meat, if you yourself haven't killed it?

9. If I go to my friend's place, can I eat from a dish that contains meat on one side of it?

10. Why do I have to obey all these rules and regulations when I don't know what will happen after death? Why should I control myself rather than enjoy the life? Why can't we remember our past lives? What will happen if I remember past lives?

11. I cannot live in this modern world without violating the five vows. What are your views?

12. We say that human life is difficult to attain, but then why is the world's population in the world is increasing? Is it because good deeds are increasing?

13. Why there are 108 beads in a rosary?

14. If Siddhas are also liberated souls, then what is the difference between Siddhas and Tirthankars?

15. I don't see a difference between Ächärya, Upadhyaya and Sädhus. They look same to me. Is that true?

16. Why there are 24 Tirthankars, and not any other number?

17. Why is there so little history available about Rishabhdev, Shantinath, Mallinath, Neminath, Parasnath, and Lord Mahävir Swami?

18. How do we know the future 24 Tirthankars?

19. What is the significance of Paryushana?

20. Why do I have to pray every day? Why do we worship Tirthankar's idol? Why do I have to worship the idol with sandal wood paste, flowers etc.? Why do people take fruits, sweets, etc. to temple?

21. Why do we need a worshipping place? Can't we do the same thing in our own home?

22. Define the dreams according to Jain religion.

23. What is the significance of the 14 dreams that mother Trishala had?

24. What do we mean by Himsä – violence?

25. What is so unique about the Non-Violence preached by Jainism?

26. What do we mean by minimizing necessary violence?

27. We are told that vegetables and animals both have lives. How can eating vegetables be less violent than eating meat?

28. Is it true that meat-eating makes people stronger and healthier?

39. Non-vegetarians argue that meat is the best source of protein. Is that true?

30. Will my being a vegetarian stop violence to animals?

31. Should we react to an attack in self-defense? Should we get rid of violent animals?

32. Some people may say: What is wrong in being a non-vegetarian if someone else does the killing?

33. Why meat-eating Europeans and Americans are more civilized, learned and powerful?

34. How does vegetarianism help ecology and the environment?

35. Is there any violence involved in using cosmetics?

36. What's wrong in wearing silk sarees or silk clothes?

37. How about the use of leather?

38. Every one knows what's wrong with the use of alcohol, but what's wrong about honey?

39. From what kind of professions should we stay away?

40. What do we mean by violence of speech and thoughts?

41. How do we stop violence of speech and thoughts?

"In all the round world there is no meat. There used to be. But now we cannot stand the thought of slaughterhouses."
— H.G. Wells (from Utopia)